HOW TO STUDY THE BIBLE AND ENJOY IT

HOW TO STUDY THE

TYNDALE HOUSE PUBLISHERS, INC., WHEATON, ILLINOIS

SKIP HEITZIG

...BIBLE AND ENJOY IT

This Billy Graham Library Selection special edition is published by the Billy Graham Evangelistic Association with permission from Tyndale House Publishers, Inc.

A **Billy Graham Library Selection** designates materials that are appropriate to a well-rounded collection of quality Christian literature, including both classic and contemporary reading and reference materials.

How to Study the Bible and Enjoy It

Designed by Dean H. Renninger

Edited by Dave Lindstedt

Published in 1996 by Connection Publishing.

Revised and expanded edition published in 2002 by Tyndale House Publishers, Inc.

Library of Congress Cataloging-in-Publication Data

Heitzig, Skip.
How to study the bible and enjoy it / Skip Heitzig.—Rev. and expanded ed.
p. cm.
ISBN 1-59328-002-5
Previous ISBN 0-8423-3723-7
1. Bible—Study and teaching. I. Title.
BS600.3.H45 2002
220′.071—dc21 2001007369

Printed in the United States of America

This volume is affectionately dedicated to

Chuck Smith,

my mentor and friend

who gave me a love for the Word of God.

His unselfish ministry and unswerving commitment

to teaching God's truths

have been a continual source of inspiration

to me through the years.

And to the wonderful people

who make up the flock of

Calvary of Albuquerque,

a church filled with people who love to

read the Word,

hear the Word,

study the Word,

and obey the Word.

It has been sheer delight

to stand week after week

and teach the Bible

to such eager and hungry hearts.

CONTENTS

1
DECIPHERING THE BIBLE

The Scriptures were not given to increase our knowledge but to change our lives. —D. L. MOODY

LET'S SUPPOSE that one day you receive a letter from a friend. You open it with eager anticipation only to discover a confusing jumble of words: "Uzza wuzza jazza wazza! Surfuss murfuss calorex flex." With a perplexed frown, you think, *Hmmm, what could this mean? A joke, perhaps? Maybe it's a secret code or some other language*. Unless someone interprets it for you, though, you are at a loss.

That's how a lot of people feel about the Bible. They see it as a confusing combination of stuffy old stories, ancient history, and irrelevant rules. "What do all those prophets, poets, and pundits have to do with me and my life today? Their world seems so—distant." They may concede that the Bible contains some noble principles—but written in archaic language that is difficult to understand. They approach the Bible like some cryptic code that needs to be broken or deciphered. Sound familiar? Some people believe they can't understand the Bible without an expert to explain its mysterious truths. They think they must go to a Bible school or seminary to *really* understand its message. Hogwash!

Of course we need to understand what the Bible says, or else it will be of little value to us, but God has taken our frailties into consideration and has given us His Word in such a way that our minds can understand its truths and our souls can be nourished by it. God *wants* us to read the Bible. He didn't intend for it to collect dust on a coffee table or lie dormant inside a desk drawer. It is a means of getting to know Him. He also wants us to understand it. It was never God's intention that the Bible become something we recite, read, chant, or sing without a thorough comprehension of its truth.

Of the many radical changes that accompany spiritual conversion, perhaps none is more significant than the shift in our attitude toward the Bible. I have experienced this personally and witnessed it in others. When a person comes into a relationship with the living God, he or she notices a hunger to know more and experience more. Who is this God? What is He like? What does He want me to do? Questions like these drive us to the Bible for answers. What a surprise, when our spiritual eyes are opened, to find that God's Word is an inexhaustible treasure chest of truth and wisdom. Better yet, it's even possible to *enjoy* studying the Bible. Has that been your experience yet?

Perhaps you've found that even though this joy of discovery is readily available to all sincere seekers, it isn't automatic. Despite the basic simplicity of the Bible's message, it isn't always easy to understand the original context of ancient Hebrew or Greek culture. On the other hand, God gave us the Bible to reveal Himself to us, and we don't have to be scholars of ancient history to enjoy a rich, rewarding, and meaningful study of the Scriptures. That's why I've written this book—to whet your appetite for studying the Bible and to give you some tools to help you properly approach a consistent study of God's Word.

Not long after I became a Christian, I went back to the church in which I'd been raised. Although it was considered a Christian denomination, Bible reading was never emphasized. As I entered the front door, Bible in hand, and made my way through the foyer, people looked at me as if I were some sort of extraterrestrial being. "Why are you bringing in one of *those things?*" someone asked. I thought, *What am I supposed to carry? A coloring book?* It dawned on me that of all the places that should welcome and foster a study of the Bible, it would be a church!

Certainly the Bible should be prominent in our churches. It is our Magna Carta, our Declaration of Independence. It is our owner's manual and our road map to life. I agree with what George Mueller, founder of the Bristol Orphanage in London during the 1800s, said about the importance of God's Word:

> The vigor of our spiritual life will be in exact proportion to the place held by the Bible in our life and thoughts. I

> solemnly state this from the experience of fifty-four years. The first three years after conversion I neglected the Word of God. Since I began to search it diligently, the blessing has been wonderful. Great has been the blessing from consecutive, diligent, daily study. I look upon it as a lost day when I have not had a good time over the Word of God.

In these chapters, I will introduce some very basic concepts that will help you feel at home just about anywhere in the Bible. You don't have to be afraid of any passage of Scripture. After all, when Jesus was still on earth, He promised His followers that He would send the Holy Spirit to teach them all things and guide them into all truth (John 16:13). The Holy Spirit is the ultimate Author of all Scripture and He is also our best interpreter. Not only did He orchestrate the composition and preservation of God's Word, He also reveals its deepest truths within our hearts. As Christians, every time we open the Bible, we can rely on the Holy Spirit to illumine the text.

IT'S ALL GREEK TO ME!

Further evidence that God intends for the Bible to be accessible to everyone is the simplicity of the language in which it was given. Greek was the most universal language at the time of the New Testament. The style in which it was written is also noteworthy. In those days, two types of Greek were spoken: a classical, refined style unique to scholars; and a simpler style, known as *koine* or common Greek, which prevailed in the Greek-speaking world from the time of Alexander the Great until about A.D. 500. This "marketplace Greek," which the average citizen could understand, was the language used by the writers of the New Testament.

That's not to suggest that all of Scripture is simplistic and easy to understand. Certainly there are difficult and controversial parts, and some verses are hard to interpret without a thorough understanding of the Bible as a whole. At times we may feel as if we are wading through a deep river. After all, we're dealing with God's infinite truth—it's not lightweight stuff! The apostle Paul even says that for now we only "know in part," but someday we'll see the full picture of truth (1 Corinthians 13:9-10). Until then, I am content to be "on hold" about some of the more difficult-to-understand issues.

I like what the great evangelist Dwight L. Moody said about the challenge of understanding the Bible:

> I am glad there's a depth in the Bible I know nothing about, for it shows its divine authorship. A man once came to me with a very difficult passage and said, "Mr. Moody, how do you explain that?"
>
> I replied, "I don't."
>
> "But how do you interpret it?"
>
> "I don't interpret it."
>
> "Well, how do you understand it?"
>
> "I don't understand it."
>
> "What do you do with it?"
>
> "I believe it! I believe many things I don't understand."

Because much of God's truth transcends us, we must be content to believe some things we don't fully understand. Nature itself is filled with wonders we cannot fathom, so how can we expect to know everything spiritual? In John 3, Jesus reminds Nicodemus that if he is unable to grasp earthly things, heavenly things would be far beyond him (John 3:12). Still, God has spoken so that we *can* understand. He delights to reveal His truth and enlighten our hearts and minds. He loves for His children to understand His ways. As Moses said, "The secret things belong to the Lord our God, but those things which are revealed belong to us and to our children forever, that we may do all the words of this law" (Deuteronomy 29:29).

In studying the Bible, don't get hung up on everything you don't understand. Instead, be content to study the Scriptures in faith, and leave the rest to God. My friend and mentor Chuck Smith once gave me some unforgettable advice: "Never give up what you *do* know for sure for what you *don't* know for sure." Great wisdom! Hold on to what you know for certain—those things that God has revealed to you in His Word. For everything else, create a little mental file titled "Waiting for Further Information" and allow God to continue to teach you. As you study, your knowledge and understanding will grow—and the "pending" file may grow as well.

DOES GOD USE HUMAN TEACHERS?

Because the Holy Spirit is ultimately the best Bible teacher, and because He resides inside every believer to direct us into God's truth, the question may arise, do we even need human teachers? I'll let the apostle Paul answer that:

> And He Himself gave some to be apostles, some prophets, some evangelists, and some pastors and teachers, for the equipping of the saints for the work of ministry, for the edifying of the body of Christ. (EPHESIANS 4:11-12)

Here's how it works: Among the many spiritual gifts that God distributes across the body of Christ, He gives the gifts of pastoring and teaching to some to help the church understand the meaning of the Scriptures. These teaching pastors are individuals used by God to equip and prepare God's people for works of service. We don't want to rely on our teachers to the detriment or exclusion of our own careful study, but there's nothing wrong with learning from others whom God has especially gifted and who have studied the original languages, history, and cultures of the Bible.

If we're not careful, though, we can become conditioned to being spoon-fed the Scriptures. After all, it's great to sit and listen to a well-versed Bible teacher and just soak it in—right? The teacher does all the work, and we do all the sitting and soaking. However, the most rewarding truths are those we discover on our own as the Holy Spirit sheds light on the Word. When we uncover truth by our own study, our convictions deepen and take root more readily than if those truths were merely handed to us. A truly gifted teacher will not only strengthen us spiritually but also whet our appetite for personal study.

The perfect balance between the enlightenment of the Holy Spirit and instruction by human teachers was perhaps modeled by the Bereans, a group of Christians that Paul met on one of his missionary journeys. He was impressed by their openness to instruction and their uncommon diligence in studying the Scriptures on their own. Paul says of the Berean believers, "These were more fair-minded than those in Thessalonica, in that they received the word with all readiness, and searched the Scriptures daily to find out whether these things were so" (Acts 17:11).

Did you notice the balance between receiving truth and searching it out? The Bereans scrutinized Paul's teaching in light of the Scriptures, and the apostle commended their actions. As a preacher myself, I advise you to listen readily to your pastor, but always check to see if his words align with what God has said in the Bible. As you become a student of the Scriptures, you will see an acceleration in your spiritual growth and you will experience the incomparable ministry of the Holy Spirit as He speaks to you directly and personally.

Perhaps you've had the same experience I've had. Maybe you've read a passage of Scripture several times without any particular insight. Then you read it again—only this time, it's like a light goes on and your understanding is clearer than ever before. Now when you refer to that Scripture, you have some genuine insight and wisdom. What happened? The Holy Spirit simply did what Jesus promised He would do—He led you into all truth.

REGULAR FEASTING ON THE WORD

One of the best habits you can develop is to read through the entire Bible on a regular basis. Before you dismiss the idea as too difficult, let me put it in perspective. It's not as formidable a task as you might think. At a very moderate rate, the entire Bible can be read in about seventy hours—about fifty-two hours for the Old Testament and eighteen hours for the New Testament. Divided over an entire year, those seventy hours equate to one hour and twenty minutes per week, or sixteen minutes per day if you were to read five days a week—or only eleven-and-a-half minutes per day if you establish the habit of reading your Bible every day. Not as time-consuming as you'd think, is it? Compare that with the time you spend on other activities. For most of us, our primary occupation consumes at least forty hours a week. Week in and week out, that's about two thousand hours annually. Each year we sleep almost three thousand hours. Add another five hundred and fifty hours per year for eating, and about fifteen hundred hours per year for watching television, and suddenly those seventy hours of Bible reading look pretty easy. Perspective is everything!

Let's take a look at some tools that can launch you into a regular, satisfying—yes, even *enjoyable*—practice of Bible reading and study.

2

FINDING THE RIGHT TOOLS

I have covenanted with my Lord that He should not send me visions or dreams or even angels. I am content with this gift of the Scriptures, which teaches and supplies all that is necessary, both for this life and that which is to come. —MARTIN LUTHER

THE RIGHT TOOLS are essential for any project. Ask anyone who has ever tried to do a job without them. When an artist sets out to express herself on canvas, she first makes sure that her palette, paints, and brushes are at hand. A carpenter knows that he needs a hammer, saw, plane, and nails to frame a house. A photographer loads film into the camera before trying to capture an image through the lens. Likewise, in studying the Bible, we need the right tools to capture God's truth in our hearts.

Let's start with the basics: The best tool for Bible study is a Bible. I know that might sound almost too obvious, but you would be surprised how many people merely study *about* the Bible rather than study the Bible itself. Some amass great libraries, thinking that commentaries and other books are essential to an adequate understanding of the Bible's message. Although many of these books may be helpful and beneficial, direct study is still the best method for reading and understanding the Bible. All other resources are secondary.

CHOOSING THE RIGHT BIBLE

The first step is to find the right Bible for you. The good news is that there are dozens of versions and styles from which to choose. Unfortunately, all the variety could make the decision more difficult. Perhaps you've already discovered the vast array of Bible translations, study systems, binding styles, print sizes, and cover colors available at your local Christian bookstore.

Which translation should you buy—the New International Version? The New American Standard Bible? The New Living Translation? The venerable King James Version? Should it be a Red Letter Edition, highlighting the words of Christ? Do you want a basic Bible—with a concordance and perhaps a few maps—or a study Bible, complete with explanatory notes, historical commentary, and a cross-reference guide? And about those references—do you prefer a side-column or center-column display? Do you want hardback, paperback, bonded leather or natural? Burgundy, black, navy, hunter green, or mauve? What began as a simple shopping trip can quickly become overwhelming. And be aware that asking someone for help in choosing a Bible may only thrust you into the middle of an ongoing debate you didn't even know existed. But don't lose heart. My goal in the next few pages is to give you a brief overview of the main decisions you'll need to make in selecting the right Bible for you.

SELECTING A TRANSLATION

Maybe you've heard the statement, "If the King James Version was good enough for the apostle Paul, it's good enough for me!" With a humorous twist this saying illustrates the intense loyalty that many people feel for the Bible they grew up with, but it also reminds us that every English version is a translation of the original text. The Old Testament was written principally in Hebrew with a few short sections in Aramaic. The letters that Paul wrote, as well as the Gospels and the rest of the New Testament, were penned in Greek—the common language of the first century. Any time the Bible is conveyed in a language other than Hebrew, Greek, and Aramaic, it is a translation. The Bible holds the distinction of having been translated into more languages—upwards of twelve hundred—than any other book in history. No English-speaking generation has been better served than ours with translations of the Bible. But how do you pick the version that's right for you? Let's start by understanding the two fundamental methods of translation.

How the Translators Do Their Job

To convert the text of the Bible from the original languages into English, translators follow one of two basic approaches: either word for word, which is sometimes called "formal equivalence"; or what is known as "dynamic equivalence," which might be best characterized as a "thought-for-thought" translation. The use of the word *equivalence* reflects the challenge of taking what is written in a host language and finding the closest corresponding word or phrase in the receptor language so that the reader is able to understand the author's intended message. I have no fewer than thirty different books in my library on the subject of Bible translations, and the only thing they all agree on is that no translation is perfect. In fact, no translation will *ever* be perfect, because in the process of transferring words, phrases, and ideas from one language into another, inevitably there will be syntax, figures of speech, and styles of expression that don't translate readily. And when the receptor language is continually in a state of flux, the translation process can be an even more formidable task.

Formal equivalence is a method of translation that attempts to give a word-for-word, clause-for-clause, and sentence-for-sentence rendering of the original text without sacrificing readability. As much as possible, the translators preserve the original syntax and express the exact meaning of the words used in the original. Examples of this more formal approach include the American Standard Version, the New American Standard Bible, and *Young's Literal Translation of the Holy Bible*. The King James Version is another example of formal equivalence, though it is not as literal as the others.

In dynamic equivalence, the translators aim for a rendering that allows the Scripture to have the same aural and emotional impact on the modern reader as it did on the ancient listener in the original language. Although dynamic equivalence often makes the text more readable for a contemporary audience, the translators must be careful not to stray into paraphrasing the text. To avoid this potential pitfall, most modern translations were compiled by teams of biblical scholars who applied their expertise in ancient culture and history to preserve the original meaning of the text. Examples of dynamic equivalent translations include the popular New International Version, the New English Bible, J. B. Phillips' *New Testament in Modern English*, and a host of others.

The development of the New Living Translation, another excellent dynamic equivalent version, demonstrates the difference between a translation and a paraphrase. In response to criticism of *The Living Bible* (a paraphrased version, popular for family devotions, that sold more than forty million copies over thirty years), the text was reviewed using several reliable ancient manuscripts and revised to create a true translation. As a result, the NLT is an easy-to-read Bible in everyday English that communicates the meaning of the original text in a refreshing and enjoyable way.

By now you might be wondering why we have so many English translations of the Bible. Are they all really necessary? Part of the answer is that our language tends to be very fluid, and because connotations of words and figures of speech continually change, the need to revise existing versions or create new ones arises periodically. Newer translations can also take advantage of the latest textual criticism and archaeological research that may shed additional light on the ancient manuscripts. Whenever a new translation is released, some will embrace it immediately, while others will prefer to stick with the familiar "tried and true." A case in point is the King James Version and the New King James Version. Although much of the language in the old King James is archaic (which is no surprise considering the work was completed in 1611), the sheer beauty and majesty of its style has kept it a favorite of many down through the ages. In 1979, the New King James Version was introduced, and it has proven to be a "reader friendly" modern English translation.

I personally prefer the New King James Version for both studying and teaching, although I often refer to other translations as well. One reason I like the NKJV is that it preserves familiar elements from the King James Bible that I began with in my earlier years. Another reason is that it seems to be a middle-of-the-road translation. Members of my congregation who are reading from a more formal translation can follow along as easily as someone using a dynamic equivalent version.

So which English version is best? A lot depends on the reader. A new Christian, for example, might choose a "dynamic equivalent" translation for its readability, whereas a seminary student might opt for a more literal rendering that holds closely to the original syntax. If your pastor teaches from a particular version that you're comfortable with, that might be a good choice.

Here's what I suggest: Find a translation you like and stick with it as your primary Bible. It should be an accurate translation and easy to read. If possible, before you buy, sit down with a few choices and compare a familiar passage of Scripture. How does it read from one version to the next? As long as you're comfortable with the version you choose, it's hard to go wrong with any of the major modern translations. Familiarize yourself with your Bible's layout and format—even the feel of its pages—until it becomes like a friend to you. The most important factor is to find a Bible that you will read regularly.

WHAT ABOUT A STUDY BIBLE?

If you've shopped for a Bible, you've probably already learned that choosing a translation is not the only decision you'll have to make. Some Bibles contain chapter outlines, introductory paragraphs, supplemental notes, and other useful information to help you quickly grasp the cultural and historical background of each book, understand the general themes of the Bible, and make practical application of the Scripture to your life. These "study Bibles" are available in most translations, and they've become quite popular. Of course, the added materials make for a bulkier Bible than a text-only version, so if size is an issue, you may want to keep your study Bible at home and carry around a slimline edition.

But should you even consider a study Bible? Is it worth the added size and possible higher price? The primary advantage of a study Bible is that it puts many useful tools at your fingertips—such as cultural, linguistic, geographical, and historical insights that may help to bridge the gap between the ancient world and our contemporary society. These available aids can help to foster a fuller understanding of biblical truth without the need to immediately purchase other resources like Bible dictionaries and commentaries. When Philip encountered the Ethiopian eunuch in the desert and heard him reading aloud from the book of Isaiah (Acts 8:26-31), he asked, "Do you understand what you are reading?" The man responded, "How can I, unless someone guides me?" A good study Bible can serve as a guide to better comprehension of the Scriptures.

Although a study Bible can be a handy tool, a word of caution is in order. Don't give in to the lure of laziness and automatically look at the printed notes at the bottom of the page rather than meditate on the passage for yourself. Keep in mind that margin notes and comments are not the inspired word of God. At best they are well-researched insights into the text, and at worst they can simply be the author's opinion or the promotion of a particular theological bent. Don't be afraid to buy a study Bible and use all the tools, just be careful not to rely on them too heavily. As you read your Bible and come to difficult passages, learn to examine the text on your own first, asking the Holy Spirit to illumine your understanding, and avoid the temptation to use the study notes as a crutch or a shortcut.

Margin Notes

When choosing a Bible, it's a good idea to find one with margin notes. These helpful references may offer a more literal translation of a word or phrase to sharpen your understanding. Some notes will include alternative renderings from comparative versions of the Bible. They can also translate the meaning of proper names from the Hebrew, Aramaic, or Greek text—insight that you wouldn't otherwise have. Another use of margin notes is to convert ancient weights and measures, distances, and monetary values into their modern equivalents.

Another common use of margin notes is to provide cross-references to passages of Scripture that will shed light on the verses you are reading. By looking up these verses, you will see how the same concept or theme is repeated elsewhere in the Bible or how another text will round out or balance the passage you are studying. Cross-references can help to expand your knowledge of Scripture and create a sense of equilibrium as you work your way through the Bible.

Paper, Binding, Cover, and Print Size

The last few decisions to make are perhaps the most personal. What kind of paper, binding, and cover do you want, and what print size is the easiest for you to read? Typestyles range from the nearly microscopic to extra large print for "more mature" eyes. The selection of materials runs the gamut from paperbacks designed to look like a "regular" book to high-quality leather covers and stitch-bound gilt-edged pages. You will quickly discover that prices rise according to the quality of the materials. As with many things in life, you get what you pay for. Hardbound Bibles, like other hardcover books, will last a long time simply because of their rugged exteriors. Soft covers may be more comfortable to open and turn the pages, but they may not be as durable.

The most important concern is usually the binding—is it sewn or merely glued? A glued binding won't last nearly as long as a stitched one will, because the pages are only attached by a thin layer of glue at the inside edge. Sewn bindings will withstand the turning of pages and flexing of the spine that normal use will bring. I suggest that you not scrimp on quality when you buy a Bible since it will become a constant companion and you'll want it to stand up under many years of solid use.

You'll also notice a variety of leather bindings, including bonded leather and genuine leather, as well as "leather-look-alike" products. The main difference between genuine and bonded leather is in the manufacturing process. Genuine leather covers are cut from solid pieces of leather, whereas bonded leather is made from leather chips bound together by latex glue. Both are good products and both will last if you take care of them. Stuffing too many church bulletins, recipes, and letters into your Bible will put an unnecessary strain on any type of binding and eventually cause it to break. Once you make your purchase, take care of your Bible. For example, don't leave it on the dashboard of your car unless you want it to resemble an ancient scrolled parchment. Respect your Bible and read it often.

A "NOTEWORTHY" SUGGESTION

The second most important study tool—after your Bible—is a notebook in which to record what God reveals to you as you read. These might be personal observations about the text, insights gleaned from a sermon, or daily devotional reflections. Some Bibles include margins wider than normal to allow readers to write notes right next to a particular passage. But whether you jot notes directly in your Bible, use a simple pad of paper, a personal journal, or the latest handheld electronic gadget, it helps to write down the thoughts and ideas that come to you while you're studying a passage of Scripture. The great evangelist Dwight L. Moody made a habit of carrying a notebook to record what he learned as he read the Bible or listened to a sermon. As you make it your practice to study God's Word, you will experience the joy of having Him directly unveil His truth and reveal His purpose in your life. Keeping some form of journal will allow you to go back and review what God has been teaching you. Writing it down helps to *remind* you of God's consistent revelation and *reinforces* the truth He conveys to your heart.

OTHER TOOLS

As you move along in your journey through the Scriptures, there are many other helpful aids that can enhance your adventure in Bible study. The sky is the limit as far as what's available, so be careful to choose wisely. If you don't, you may find yourself up to your neck in unused books and unpaid bills from the bookstore. The last thing you need is an impressive set of theology books that winds up as an expensive doorstop! That's not to say there aren't valuable resources available to enhance your biblical knowledge. Here are a few key references to consider:

Concordance

Have you ever scratched your head and said to yourself, *Where is that verse that talks about* guidance? *It's gotta be somewhere in the Old*

Testament—but how can I find it? That's when a concordance—one of the most basic and best tools for Bible study—really comes in handy. A concordance is an alphabetized index of words used in the Bible with a listing of verses where each word appears. It enables you to find a specific passage even if you can only remember a key word or two. In addition to the Scripture reference, each entry includes a short excerpt from the verse where that word occurs. Some also come equipped with short definitions of each Bible word translated from the original languages. This inexpensive tool can be used to trace a theme throughout the Bible or do word studies.

Many Bibles come with a partial concordance in the back, but their usefulness is limited by the fact that they don't include every word or every instance where a word appears. If you want an "exhaustive" concordance that lists *every* word in the Bible and *every* place where that word appears, they are available in print and software. *Strong's*, *Young's*, and *Cruden's* are all excellent choices. Charles Spurgeon, the great Victorian preacher, wrote in the flyleaf of his *Cruden's* concordance, "For these ten years this has been the book at my left hand when the Word of God has been at my right." *Strong's*, *Young's*, and *Cruden's* are all keyed to the King James Version, but nowadays you can find a concordance keyed to almost any version of the Bible. Today's computer technology has made compiling such works much easier and faster. If you're able to purchase additional tools to enhance your personal Bible study, put a good concordance at the top of your list. You'll find it to be a good navigational tool. Just be sure to match the concordance to the version of the Bible you will use most often.

Bible Dictionary

A good Bible dictionary is another resource that will help to unlock the contents of Scripture. As the name implies, a Bible dictionary defines words, topics, names, and places in the Bible. Most consist of brief articles, arranged alphabetically, containing a summary of information about various subjects, as well as information from other historical sources. Usually contained in a single volume, Bible dictionaries are a general and topical reference suitable for readers with little or no formal training in biblical history or languages. They are intended to sharpen your focus on a biblical theme and give you an essential grasp of the subject you are studying. Many Bible dictionaries contain great photographs, reference maps, and even small atlases, so you can get a general feel for particular locations. Because most Bible dictionaries are compiled by a variety of contributors, you can expect to receive well-rounded information about many Bible subjects. Again, there are many fine dictionaries from which to choose, so your best bet is to spend some time comparing them—or ask your local bookstore proprietor to help you select one.

Commentaries

Throughout the history of the church many well-known and respected theologians have undertaken the task of writing commentaries on the Bible to help others in interpreting and understanding the Scriptures. As with any book, the quality of a Bible commentary depends on the skill and insight of the author. Well-written commentaries reflect hours of careful research by scholars who have invested themselves in studying the original languages, ancient history and culture, and the overall scope and message of the Bible. A good commentary will provide useful insight without bogging you down with technicalities, and it will help you focus on application of the text—what the verses mean to you personally.

Because commentaries can be fairly expensive, take the time to familiarize yourself with what's available, and choose the best one you can find for your specific purpose. Some commentaries run to several volumes (and even multiple volumes for a single book of the Bible), but it is possible to find reputable single- or two-volume sets that encompass the entire Bible. But don't be too quick to start building a library. You don't want to lean too heavily on commentaries for your understanding of Scripture, lest you become dependent on them and lose your love for digging into the Bible for yourself. There's nothing like gaining your own insight firsthand. Keep in mind that the Holy Spirit is still the best teacher. Other people's comments are simply that—their comments. As one person put it, "There is no substitute for reading the Bible; it throws a great deal of light on the commentaries!" Make it your practice to go right to the source and skip the middleman as much as possible.

Computer Resources

The rapid growth of computer technology has revolutionized the field of personal Bible study. What the Gutenberg press was to communication in the fifteenth century, computers have become in our contemporary age. Stand-alone computer programs, via CD-ROM, and on-line access have greatly improved the Bible student's ability to view a variety of valuable resources very quickly. The benefits of using computer technology are thoroughness and speed. A computer can search for verses and words in several versions of the Bible and in multiple other books all at one time. With the click of a mouse or the touch of a key you can have language, themes, maps, and more, literally at your fingertips. If you're not computer savvy, these programs can be a bit intimidating at first, but with a little patience you can learn how to get the most out of these tools.

All computer programs have benefits and limitations. If you're not already set up with a well-equipped computer, the first limitation may be price. You'll need enough available memory and speed to handle the demands of some of these software packages. The software itself may also be pricey, although most companies offer their programs in pieces or "modules" that allow you to start with a basic package and upgrade as you go. Also, once you have purchased a computer, the cost of the software is usually far less than buying the same resources in print.

THE LAST WORD

Here's the bottom line on Bible study tools: I have traveled in many parts of the world where even the best-equipped pastors have only a study Bible, a concordance, and perhaps a Bible dictionary. Three or four books at most—and no computer resources at all! These pastors have learned how to study the Scriptures inductively on their own, without relying on commentaries or other tools. It is interesting to note that most of the church growth worldwide is currently occurring in these third-world countries. Clearly, having a huge library of books is not the most important factor. You can buy the best Bible study tools available and still not be a good Bible student.

I don't mean to downplay the usefulness of these many resources (and certainly in the United States we are blessed to have so much help available), but I do want to emphasize the importance of desiring "the pure milk of the word" (1 Peter 2:2). The benefit you gain by learning to study the Bible (and enjoy it!) on your own will far outweigh the comments, insights, and opinions of even the most learned theologian. The purpose of this book is to show you how to make your own observations of Scripture and your own application of God's truth.

3

GETTING STARTED

YOU HAVE YOUR BIBLE, your concordance and Bible dictionary are nearby, you've opened your notebook, and you're ready to begin. Now what? How can you get the most out of your Bible study?

First let me ask you a very basic question: *How hungry are you?* Having the right tools is important, of course, but spiritual hunger is the driving force behind effective Bible study. As I see it, there is a big difference between simply *reading* the Bible and truly *feeding* on God's Word.

Have you ever read a particular passage of Scripture several times yet still felt as if you were missing the full impact of the message? Then one day you read an article or hear a sermon on the same verses and suddenly the Bible comes alive. It's like someone turned on the lights in a pitch-black room. You're amazed at how the author or speaker was able to glean so much more from the same passage of Scripture and you wonder, *What happened when I read those verses? How could I miss so much?*

There are many reasons why we miss the fullness of truth in God's Word. One is the incredible depth that God has built into the Scriptures. Other factors include the stage of our spiritual development, our understanding of the Bible as a whole, our willingness to wait and listen to the Lord's voice, our preoccupation with other issues, and even the daily stress of life. But let me encourage you: You *can* understand the Bible if you really want to. The fact that you're reading this book shows you are concerned about learning more and going deeper in your study of the Bible. That in itself is a sign of spiritual vitality. God's own Word tells us that God rewards "those who diligently seek Him" (Hebrews 11:6), and He will respond to your heartfelt desire to learn more about Him.

FIND THE RIGHT TIME

To start, find a quiet place and set aside a regular time to study your Bible and meet with God. As with getting to know any other person, the more time you spend together the better you'll get to know Him. And you'll discover that the Bible is a great "conversation starter." Some people find that early morning is the best time to study, because everything is fresh and the day starts off right. Others prefer the evening or late at night when everyone else is in bed. Find what works best for you. There are no rules here. What's important is that you set aside time to be alone with the Lord—a time when other voices and needs aren't competing for your attention. These "quiet times" will forge your spiritual understanding, deepen your intimacy with God, and sharpen your discernment. Whether it's morning, noon, or night, the time you spend with the Lord will become the foundation of your day. Make it a time you look forward to, and guard it carefully.

CULTIVATE THE RIGHT HEART

Before we can fully grasp the truth of the Bible, our spiritual senses must be awakened. It isn't enough to merely understand a bunch of historical or factual information if the inner core of our being hasn't been touched. How often have you heard someone lament after a quick reading of Scripture, "I don't get it! Every time I try to read the Bible, it just doesn't make any sense"? Of course, there may be many reasons for such a response. Certainly there are difficult sections of Scripture that are hard for anyone to understand. We've also discussed how the Bible translation one chooses may affect comprehension. But sometimes the answer is simply that the reader has yet to be spiritually awakened. In order for God's truth to be ascertained, a change from within—a spiritual rebirth—must happen first (see John 3:3-12). As the apostle Paul says in 1 Corinthians 2:14, "People who aren't Christians can't understand these truths from God's Spirit. It all sounds foolish to them because only those who have the Spirit can understand what the Spirit means" (NLT).

Appetites are strong motivators. When we're hungry, we want to eat. However, if we were to set up a hamburger stand outside of a four-star restaurant and try to convince diners who were leaving after their meals to buy a hamburger, we wouldn't have much luck. Why? Because their appetite has been satisfied by the food they just ate and they're no longer hungry. If we want people to eat our burgers, we might want to set up in front of a construction site where the workers are sweating off the calories and building up an appetite. By the same token, spiritually hungry people will find studying the Bible invigorating and satisfying—unless they've been filling up on the "junk food" our society offers, like an over-busy schedule, too much popular entertainment, or the countless other diversions that can sate one's spiritual appetite. The apostle Peter admonishes us to "crave pure spiritual milk so that you can grow into the fullness of your salvation. Cry out for this nourishment as a baby cries for milk" (1 Peter 2:2, NLT).

A good perspective to adopt when reading the Bible is that of an obedient servant waiting for instruction from the master. When the attitude of our heart reflects a readiness to hear and respond, the text of the Bible comes alive. The adventure of following God's will takes on a whole new complexion when we stop to listen and then act upon what we hear. The young prophet Samuel's response to God is a good example. When God got his attention, Samuel responded appropriately: "Speak, for Your servant hears" (1 Samuel 3:10). It isn't enough just to be a Christian, if you aren't an obedient one. If the Bible seems dry and unexciting, check your attitude. Is your heart conditioned to listen and obey?

TAKE THE RIGHT APPROACH

Down through the ages, readers have approached the Scriptures from every conceivable angle. Some, like the medieval Jewish cabalists, have taken a mystical perspective that treats the Bible like a collection of esoteric mysteries to be deciphered. Others focus on an academic understanding of the text, context, and historical accuracy of Scripture. Many have appreciated the Bible for its devotional aspects—how the truth can be applied to our lives. Still others focus on how God has revealed Himself through His word. Is there one "right" way to study the Bible? Is there a standard method we should adopt or a particular order we should follow? Which is the best technique? I recommend two basic approaches to studying the Bible:

1. Read it like any other book.
2. Read it *unlike* any other book.

The first way to read the Bible is like we would any other book. If we were reading an autobiography, for example, we would focus on what the author revealed about himself or herself. We would evaluate statements and events in light of what we already knew about the period when the author lived, and we would be looking for new insights. Likewise, when we read a book from the Bible, we should seek to understand the author and his message in the context of ancient history and culture. When we read a book that has been translated from another language—such as Plato's *Republic* or Dostoyevsky's *Crime and Punishment*—we naturally want to know how well it has been translated and how it was understood by its original audience. Has the translator captured the precise definitions of words and the flavor of idiomatic expressions? As we seek to understand the author's intent, we must avoid imposing our own interpretation onto the real meaning. The same is true when we read historical books. If we are studying a book on European culture during the Renaissance, it helps to understand the perspective of people who lived on the Continent during that time. So it is with the Bible. When we consider the importance of language, culture, and context, our understanding is enhanced and we can save ourselves from painful misinterpretations and misrepresentations of the text.

We should also study the Bible *unlike* any other book. It is, after all, the living Word of God and should be treated as such. We must interact closely with this "book of books," allowing our lives to be examined by the piercing white light of its probing truth. We wouldn't study an algebra textbook or a volume of American history—or even a book of philosophy—and expect it to change our lives the way the Bible can. Unlike other books, we don't read the Bible merely for information. Instead, we seek to respond to its commands, heed its warnings, and apply its precepts to our lives. We want to be encouraged by its promises, corrected by its admonitions, and transformed by its amazing truth.

Shaking the Tree

If we're going to "lay hold on the Bible until the Bible lays hold on us," as Will Houghton suggested, we need to have a plan. If our method is random and haphazard—what I call "reading and raking," where we scratch the surface of the Scriptures and pay attention to whatever strikes our fancy—our results will also be random and haphazard. Before long, we'll encounter some "hard ground" where the raking isn't so easy, and if we're not careful, our Bible study will soon degenerate into an intermittent exercise without much satisfaction. Jesus told His followers to "consider carefully how you listen" (Luke 8:18, NIV), so let's devise a plan to consider carefully the truth of Scripture.

Martin Luther said that he studied the Bible the same way he gathered apples. First he shook the whole tree so that the ripest fruit would fall to the ground. Then he climbed the tree and shook each limb. After he had shaken each limb, he shook each branch, and then every twig. Finally, just to make sure he hadn't missed any good apples, he looked under each leaf.

We can "shake the tree" by reading the Bible the same way we would read any other book, perusing the text at normal reading speed and enjoying the full scope of the story. Along the way, we're bound to pick up a bushel or two of spiritual apples: truth, wisdom, and insight into the character of God. Once we've read through the Scriptures as a whole, we can go back and "shake every limb," studying the individual books of the Bible. As we proceed, we can "shake every branch," focusing our attention chapter by chapter (as long as the chapter breaks don't interfere with the flow of the argument, which occasionally happens). Continuing to narrow our focus and searching for deeper truths, we "shake every twig" by carefully studying individual paragraphs and sentences. And some of the most rewarding (and *tasty*) fruit can be found when we "look under every leaf" by searching for the meaning of specific words and phrases. "Harvesting" the Word of God in this manner provides a great balance and helps to keep our study interesting and enjoyable.

As you systematically study God's Word, you will begin to form a framework of truth by which to live. This grid will help you make decisions and discern between what is best and what is merely good. This process doesn't happen overnight, but as you weave God's truth into the fabric of your personality, you will transform your life forever. You'll find that your perspective becomes clearer and more stable as you add to your spiritual knowledge "precept upon precept, line upon line" (Isaiah 28:10). The truth will liberate you as it confronts old habits and exposes your inner motives. You'll become wiser as you learn both what is pleasing and displeasing to God.

Reading and Retaining

It's a fact of our humanity that we retain only a small percentage of what we read. If we want to increase our retention—and ultimately our understanding—we must interact with what we read until it becomes a part of us. I've found that a simple, three-step process can greatly enhance our comprehension and retention. These easy-to-follow steps are *observation*, *interpretation*, and *application*. I suggest you commit them to memory right now.

Observation is simply *opening your eyes* to what the text is saying. If you skim too quickly, you'll overlook important details. Take time to read and reread the text until it becomes familiar. Observe everything you can and make a note of certain things that stand out: Who is writing this? Who was the original audience for this information? What is the setting? What time did it happen? Who is involved?

Interpretation involves *opening your mind* to what the text means. Review your observations, paying attention to key words, themes, and principles. It may also help to paraphrase the text (rewriting it on paper or in your mind). As you put the passage in your own words, you'll move beyond the facts and begin to grasp the *meaning* of the text.

When you *open your heart* to what the text means *to you* and start to personalize the truths you uncover in Scripture, you've begun the process of *application*. The focus here is on what God is saying to you specifically through what you have read. Is He calling you to stop some behavior or change your attitude about something? Is He inspiring you to start living in a particular way? Is He calling you to a more intimate relationship with Him? As you assimilate the principles, prohibitions, commands, and encouragements found in Scripture, God's Word will come alive.

Once you start reading the Bible with these three steps in mind, they will become second nature to you. You'll find yourself retaining more of what you read and enjoying your study more! Whenever you read your Bible, whether it's at home, at work, or at the local coffee shop, you can observe, interpret, and apply God's word to your life's situations. As you do, an amazing transformation will take place. You'll find yourself becoming a different kind of person. Old habits will be dropped and new ones developed. You'll be changed. You'll be hooked. You'll be excited.

HOW TO BEGIN STUDYING

In order to help you put into practice the basic pattern we have established of observation, interpretation, and application, I'd like to suggest three simple ways to approach the Scriptures—three modes of study—that have proven effective: *devotional*, *systematic*, and *topical*. These aren't rigid categories, and one isn't necessarily better—or more spiritual—than another. Each has its merits, and they can easily be combined to suit your desires. One approach may work for a season, only to be replaced by another later on. Stay flexible and allow the Spirit of the Lord to guide you.

Reading Devotionally

Devotional Bible study is the process of reflecting on a few verses or a passage of Scripture and making a personal application. Many Christians refer to this worshipful way of reflecting on the Scriptures as "having a quiet time" or "having devotions." Although devotional study is not primarily an academic approach to the Bible, it doesn't mean that we bypass observation or interpretation on our way to application. Instead, we are simply endeavoring to encounter God on the holy ground of His word by "stepping through the veil" into His presence to commune with Him. Devotional study is a peaceful and reassuring way to begin or end your day. Rather than examining the Bible as simply a textbook, as we might in school, devotional study focuses on seeking the Lord and desiring to know His will as it applies to us. The knowledge of the *book* is not as important in this method as knowing the *author* of the book. Time spent in devotional Bible study becomes a joyful rendezvous with God.

Countless books and periodicals are available to supplement a devotional approach to Bible study. Most will suggest a portion of Scripture to focus on each day and offer comments or a brief narrative to guide your meditation. *Our Daily Bread* and *The Daily Life* are two good examples of widely distributed devotional periodicals. Devotional books, such as Oswald Chambers's *My Utmost For His Highest* or Charles Spurgeon's *Morning and Evening*, focus on one verse followed by a full devotional for the day. Although these publications are excellent and meaningful, don't let them become the only way you read the Bible. If you do, you'll cheat yourself out of the joy of digging into the meat of the Word on your own. Learn to go beyond the published devotionals and right into the Bible for yourself. The thrill and lasting value of your own discovery will far outweigh what someone else has written.

Reading Systematically

One of the most effective ways to study the Scriptures is to go through the Bible—all sixty-six books—chapter by chapter, verse by verse, and word by word. I'm not advocating that you try this all in one sitting, of course, nor do you need to start with Genesis 1 and read the books in strict order through Revelation. But it is important that you expose yourself to the "full counsel" of Scripture and not avoid certain books just because you think they might be dry or difficult. The key to successfully reading through the whole Bible is to break up the reading into manageable sections and balance your reading across the various types of literature contained in the Bible. Let me suggest the following seven-day plan:

(SUNDAY: Read the passage of Scripture that your pastor is preaching from. You can do this either before or after church and it will reinforce the message and keep you on track with your own congregation.

(MONDAY: Read from the *legal* books (Genesis to Deuteronomy). These five books of Moses comprise the Jewish *Torah* (or the law). Also known as the *Pentateuch* (meaning five scrolls), these books describe the events from Creation until the time when Moses dies and Israel is about to enter the Promised Land.

(TUESDAY: Read from the *historical* books (Joshua to Esther), which recount the history of the nation of Israel, God's covenant people. The rise and fall of Israel's theocracy, its captivity in foreign lands, and its return to Palestine are all covered in these books.

(WEDNESDAY: Read from the *poetic* books (Job to the Song of Solomon). These books are often referred to as the *wisdom books* because they contain highly practical lessons expressed through Hebrew poetry.

(THURSDAY: Read from the *prophetic* books (Isaiah to Malachi). These writings describe the ministries of various prophets who were sent by God to warn Israel or to speak to spiritually slumbering or disobedient nations on God's behalf. These prophecies were often fulfilled in the prophet's own day, or later in biblical history (such as the prophecies concerning the coming of Messiah and the fall of Jerusalem), and some are still awaiting fulfillment in the future (such as prophecies concerning the second coming of Christ and the end of the age).

(FRIDAY: Read from the *Gospels* (Matthew, Mark, Luke, and John). These four accounts tell of the ancestry, birth, life, ministry, death, and resurrection of the Bible's main character—Jesus Christ. They reveal His dual nature as both man and God. Together they present a well-rounded perspective of the Messiah.

(SATURDAY: Read from the rest of the New Testament (Acts to Revelation), which includes the history of the early church, various letters that were sent to them by the apostles, and a description of the earth's upcoming final days.

When you stop each day, place a marker wherever you are and pick up your reading of that section on the same day the next week. This plan will inject enough variety into your reading to keep you looking forward to the next session. Using this method, you can read through the Bible consistently, taking long or short portions and covering as much ground as you like. If you read about four chapters per day, you will complete the entire Bible in nine or ten months. But don't feel guilty if you don't read through several chapters in one sitting. Take your time and don't forget the basic steps of observation, interpretation, and application. (I will explain this process in the next few chapters.)

If you prefer not to use the suggested seven-day plan, many Bibles have a daily schedule in the back that will guide you through the Bible in a year. Whatever you do, don't be one of the many Christians who, sadly, has never once read through the entire Bible. Instead, commit yourself to the wonderful journey of "walking through the Word" over the next nine to twelve months.

Reading Topically

Another practical approach to Bible study is to settle on one idea or topic and study everything the Bible has to say about it. To study the concept of *grace*, for example, you would use a concordance to find every passage in the Bible where the word *grace* appears and then read the surrounding verses to develop and deepen your understanding. By concentrating on a single topic rather than a systematic verse-by-verse study, you will uncover the "full counsel of Scripture" on that particular subject, which can then guide your personal application. And whereas a systematic study will show you the scope and sequence of God's revelation, a topical approach provides an "in-depth" look at Bible themes, revealing how they emerge with more definition through the ages. For example, in the Old Testament God commanded Israel not to eat pork, but in the New Testament He makes allowance for His people to eat all things, as long as it is with a thankful heart and doesn't cause another believer to stumble (1 Timothy 4:3; 1 Corinthians 8:13).

Although a topical approach can be a very insightful way to study the Scriptures, it can also cause us to become a bit imbalanced. How? Simply because in choosing topics that are important or interesting to *us*, we may overlook or neglect other important truths that might counterbalance our particular viewpoint. A topical study could well be compared to an appetizer in a restaurant: It's a great way to whet the appetite for a more complete and comprehensive study of the entire Bible. By *combining* a topical approach with a systematic study, you will cover the major themes of the Bible *in context*, and you'll be better able to see the emphasis that God has placed on each topic within the text.

Sounds Great, but Where Can I Find the Time?

If all this sounds like a pretty steep order—and you're wondering, *Who's got that kind of time?*—give me another minute to make my case. It's true that studying the Bible will take thought, effort, and commitment—as well as time. Believe me, I know that time is a precious commodity these days. Our schedules are already overloaded with work, family and friends, sleep, and recreation. But have you ever noticed that we tend to make time for things that are really important to us? Somehow, even with all the demands placed on us in our crazy-paced age, we manage to have hobbies, see movies, and go to sporting events. If your days are filled with scheduled events and meetings with all sorts of "important" people, do yourself a favor and schedule a daily appointment with God. Write it in your daily planner! I'd say that God's a pretty important person to meet with, wouldn't you? Let's both make those meetings a priority. When we get right down to it, we can live more simply by stripping away the many activities that really are not as important as they seem. Here's a sobering statistic: In 1989, Americans purchased Harlequin romance novels at the rate of 7,191 per hour. Can you imagine what would happen if God's people would show a similar interest in His Word? Let's face it. If you're too busy to spend time with God—it could be that you're just too busy!

Don't let your Bible end up as just another decoration on your living-room coffee table. Turn it loose to do its work in your life. I guarantee that your Bible will speak to you—if you let it. Of course, it's God's voice that speaks through every verse, but I wonder, if your Bible had a voice of its own and could talk to you from its leather-bound covers—what would it say? Maybe it would whisper something like this:

I would like a job as tutor, teacher, and advisor to your family.

I will never take a vacation. I will never be out of humor.

I don't drink or smoke. I won't borrow your clothes or raid your refrigerator.

I will be up in the morning as early as anyone in the household, and I will stay up as late as you wish.

I will help solve any problems your children might have. I will give you the satisfaction of knowing that no question your child asks will go unanswered. For that matter, I will answer any of your own questions on subjects that range from "How did we get here?" to "Where are we headed?"

I will help settle disputes and differences of opinion. I will give you information that will help you with your job, your family, and all of your other interests.

In short, I will give you the knowledge that will ensure the continued success of your family.

I am your Bible. Do I get the job?

4

OBSERVATION: OPENING YOUR EYES

Scripture knowledge is the candle without which faith cannot see to do its work. —ANONYMOUS

ACCORDING TO THE *Encyclopedia Britannica*, the Bible is the all-time best-seller in the English-speaking world, unequaled by any other book ever published. The Guinness organization says that the Bible is not only the world's best-selling book, but also the most widely distributed book ever, with an estimated 2.5 billion copies sold since 1815. Not only that, but it has been translated into 2,233 languages and dialects.

Of course, sales figures and the number of copies in print don't tell the full story. There's a big difference between merely owning a Bible (or two) and allowing the truth revealed in its pages to have an impact on your life. Even though the Bible is the best-selling book of all time and the most outstanding piece of literature ever written, many people who own one know little or nothing about it. They haven't yet discovered that the real joy comes in understanding God's Word and being transformed by its timeless truths.

Several years ago, *National Review* magazine published an article of bloopers gathered from a test given to a group of high school students about some fairly well-known Bible stories. These genuine and unretouched renditions illustrate how easily our minds can jumble the facts and leave us with an obscure version of the Scriptures. For example, in the first book of the Bible, Guinnesses, God got tired of creating the world, so He took the Sabbath off. Adam and Eve were created from an apple tree. Noah's wife was called Joan of Ark. Lot's wife was a pillar of salt by day and a ball of fire by night. The seventh commandment is *Thou shalt not admit adultery*. Moses died before he ever reached Canada, and Joshua led the Hebrews in the battle of Geritol. David was a Hebrew king skilled at playing the liar. Solomon had three hundred wives and seven hundred porcupines. Samson was a strongman who slayed the Philistines with the ax of the apostles.

Certainly, these are honest mistakes, and no one can be expected to remember every detail of every Bible story. Not even the most mature Christian is a walking concordance. But the greater point here is about our powers of observation. Sometimes when we read the Bible we simply don't "see" it—that is, we make no significant observations about what we have read. Observation is one of the most helpful skills we can acquire.

When we learn how to examine the text and retain what we see, and then use that information to help us interpret and apply what we've read, our Bible study experience becomes much more enjoyable. The rewards come when we develop "handles" to mentally take hold of the truth.

We've all had a similar experience when meeting someone new. We smile, shake hands, exchange names and discuss bits of information, smile a bit more, then go our separate ways. If someone were to ask us later to describe the person we had met, many of us would have a hard time recalling very many details. We might remember certain aspects, but unless we have a photographic memory (or we somehow made mental notes about the person's clothing, facial features, and hairstyle), we'd be hard-pressed to give an accurate composite description. We met. We spoke. We saw. We shook hands. But we didn't *observe*.

If you want to improve your powers of observation, here's a little game you can play. The next time you're at the grocery store with someone, walk down an aisle together and silently notice what's there. Once you've left the aisle, discuss how many different items you saw during your walk-through. Describe products, sizes, and colors. Were there more boxes, cans, or bottles on the shelves? How many bottles did you see? What size were the containers? How many shelves were used in the display? How many empty spaces did you see? Which products belonged on those shelves? Compare your answers and then walk back down the aisle to see who observed more. You will be amazed at what you saw and what you missed!

"OPEN MY EYES, LORD"

Another way to sharpen our observation skills—and one we too often overlook—is simply to ask the Lord to open our eyes to the Scriptures. As we seek to understand the truth revealed in the Bible, we have the privilege of coming humbly before the divine author and asking the Holy Spirit to bring illumination to our hearts. King David, whom God inspired to write many of the Psalms, offers this prayer in Psalm 119:18: "Open my eyes, that I may see wondrous things from Your law." Following David's example, perhaps you could begin your study with a prayer something like this:

> Lord, I submit myself to You as Your servant. I pray that You would speak to me personally as I now open Your Word. Sharpen my powers of observation and open my eyes to what the text is saying. Give me wisdom and insight as I seek to interpret what the text means. And help me to apply Your truth to the specific areas in my life that need Your touch. Gently convict me of any issues I'm neglecting or trying to hide. Lord, I give You complete permission to search my heart to see if there is anything in me that is contrary to Your will. Challenge me with Your holiness and comfort me with Your promises, in Jesus' name. Amen.

As you proceed with your study, continue to bathe the entire process in prayer. Inevitably you'll come to some difficult portions of Scripture that you don't understand. When that happens, stop and pray for insight and discernment. Cry out for wisdom and understanding, and God will answer you.

> *My son, if you receive my words,*
> *And treasure my commands within you,*
> *So that you incline your ear to wisdom,*
> *And apply your heart to understanding;*
> *Yes, if you cry out for discernment,*
> *And lift up your voice for understanding,*
> *If you seek her as silver,*
> *And search for her as for hidden treasures;*
> *Then you will understand the fear of the* LORD,
> *And find the knowledge of God.* (PROVERBS 2:1-5)

Finish your time of Bible study by thanking God for the insight He has given you. Presenting yourself to God as an empty vessel, eager to be filled, is the single most effective step you can take in understanding and applying the truths of the Bible. The great preacher R. W. Dale noted that, "Study without prayer is atheism, and prayer without study is presumption." We need both prayer and study.

OBSERVATION LEVEL ONE: A FLYOVER VIEW

There is nothing quite like seeing the Grand Canyon from twenty thousand feet in the air. I remember the first time I caught a glimpse of this vast national landmark from a jet window on a transcontinental flight. In the context of the surrounding landscape, the enormity of this magnificent chasm, basking in the afternoon sunlight, was dramatically displayed like I had never seen it before. Later, when I visited the canyon, I appreciated it much more up close because of the perspective I had gained by having seen it from afar.

The same principle can be applied to our study of Scripture. We will gain much more from our detailed, verse-by-verse study if we have first observed the overall "landscape" of the text by reading—in its entirety, in one sitting if possible—the particular book of the Bible we are studying. Of course, that's easier to do with some books than with others. Most of the shorter New Testament books, like James, 1 John, or Philemon, and the books of the minor prophets in the Old Testament, can easily be read in one sitting, because they're nice and concise. But there are quite a few books that are much longer and more formidable. To read Isaiah all at once, for example, would require a huge chunk of time or an Evelyn Wood speed-reading course. My suggestion with the longer books is to break them up over a few days. If you were reading Romans, for example, which has sixteen chapters, you might read five chapters one day, five the next, and then six chapters on the third day. Spreading out the reading keeps your load manageable without undermining your momentum. As you read, jot down your observations along with key words and any questions that come to mind, but don't get bogged down with this. You want to keep your reading at a steady flow in order to get the "flyover view."

Let me suggest another way to gain a broad perspective of the larger books: Try reading just the headings and the first sentence or two of each section. This technique is not as revealing as reading the entire book, but it will enable you to observe the overall context of the book, to see how it flows and where it is going, in a relatively short amount of time—much like seeing the Bible from twenty thousand feet. You'll be able to scan the general topography and note the major landmarks. You'll taxi through the introduction, take off in the first few chapters, and soar over the main body of the text. By the time you land on the closing chapter, you'll have a general feel for the entire message and structure of the passage. It may be a quick flight, but a lot of information can be gleaned in this way before you return to walk the terrain more slowly at ground level. To prepare for what we'll discuss in the remainder of this chapter, practice this skimming technique using the first few chapters of the Gospel of Mark.

OBSERVATION LEVEL TWO: A GROUND-LEVEL VIEW

Once you have completed your "flyover" of the entire book, it's time to go back through the specific passage you've chosen to study and take a "ground-level" view. The first step in this "walking tour" is simply to observe what's there. To help you focus as you read, ask the six basic questions that any journalist would ask—What? When? Where? How? Who? and Why?—to discover the essential facts of the story. When you apply these questions to the study of the Bible, you will uncover information that leads you into a deeper understanding of God's Word. It isn't necessary to find the answers to all six questions in every passage, but the more you find, the more rewarding the exercise will be. Once you've established this pattern of investigation, you will automatically ask these same questions every time you read the Bible, which will deepen your level of study and broaden your range of understanding.

As you observe, don't lose yourself in the details. Sometimes you may sense the Holy Spirit "pressing" a certain truth upon you—and it's important to be sensitive to those promptings—but otherwise try to divide your time proportionately across the entire passage or section you are studying. This will keep you "balanced" as well as stimulate you to enjoy parts of the Bible that you might ordinarily skip over.

Also, don't get hung up on all the steps you have to remember. It may appear at this point that we're only making Bible reading more complicated, which translates into being less enjoyable. Not so! After a while these instructional steps will become second nature to you and you'll find the Bible becoming more interesting and much more pleasurable to read. It's sort of like learning a new sport—like golf. At first the instruction seems laborious and cumbersome—standing just so and placing your hands in a gnarled and unnatural position. It feels awkward to swing the club while bending one arm and keeping the other arm straight. Coordinating the movement of your feet, hips, upper body, and head in sync with the swing of the club is anything but comfortable; it seems downright impossible. But soon it all comes together. Eventually the new method is locked into muscle memory and you're on your way to a lifetime of enjoyment. Though there will be times of frustration along the way, the game becomes more and more rewarding.

It's the same with Bible reading. The more thoroughly you learn the right approach, the more you'll experience the satisfaction of personal discovery.

Let's take a "ground-level" view of Mark 1:1-20. After you've read through the passage, open your notebook and ask the six basic questions.

> The beginning of the gospel of Jesus Christ, the Son of God. As it is written in the Prophets:
>
> "Behold, I send My messenger before Your face, Who will prepare Your way before You." "The voice of one crying in the wilderness: 'Prepare the way of the Lord; make His paths straight.'"
>
> John came baptizing in the wilderness and preaching a baptism of repentance for the remission of sins. Then all the land of Judea, and those from Jerusalem, went out to him and were all baptized by him in the Jordan River, confessing their sins. Now John was clothed with camel's hair and with a leather belt around his waist, and he ate locusts and wild honey. And he preached, saying, "There comes One after me who is mightier than I, whose sandal strap I am not worthy to stoop down and loose. I indeed baptized you with water, but He will baptize you with the Holy Spirit."
>
> It came to pass in those days that Jesus came from Nazareth of Galilee, and was baptized by John in the Jordan. And immediately, coming up from the water, He saw the heavens parting and the Spirit descending upon Him like a dove.

> Then a voice came from heaven, "You are My beloved Son, in whom I am well pleased."
>
> Immediately the Spirit drove Him into the wilderness. And He was there in the wilderness forty days, tempted by Satan, and was with the wild beasts; and the angels ministered to Him.
>
> Now after John was put in prison, Jesus came to Galilee, preaching the gospel of the kingdom of God, and saying, "The time is fulfilled, and the kingdom of God is at hand. Repent, and believe in the gospel."
>
> And as He walked by the Sea of Galilee, He saw Simon and Andrew his brother casting a net into the sea; for they were fishermen. Then Jesus said to them, "Follow Me, and I will make you become fishers of men." They immediately left their nets and followed Him. When He had gone a little farther from there, He saw James the son of Zebedee, and John his brother, who also were in the boat mending their nets. And immediately He called them, and they left their father Zebedee in the boat with the hired servants, and went after Him.

Now jot down your observations as you work your way through the six journalistic questions. Like an investigator who arrives on the scene after an incident has occurred, you are trying to determine exactly what is going on in the passage. Not everything you read and notice will be of equal importance in learning the vital meaning of the passage. But you'll soon learn what's important and what can be passed over. Your diligence, along with prayerful dependence on the Holy Spirit, will soon yield spiritual treasures that you'll enjoy for a lifetime.

1. WHAT? There are a number of ways to phrase this question, but let's look at three examples:

What happened in the story? A man identified as God's messenger came dressed in unusual clothing with a penetrating call to repentance. He was baptizing people to symbolize their repentance. While he was baptizing one man in particular (Jesus), heaven opened and God spoke. Immediately after His baptism, Jesus was driven into the wilderness for forty days, where Satan tempted Him. Meanwhile, the messenger was thrown in jail. Jesus then returned to Galilee and began to gather a group of followers.

What are the main ideas expressed? The first idea is the fulfillment of an ancient prophecy. John and Jesus were part of a long-awaited plan to bring the kingdom of God to earth. Another idea is that of repentance from sin. Then we have the description of Jesus bringing the Holy Spirit, being tempted by Satan, and ministered to by angels. Finally, the idea of dropping one occupation to take up another is a central concept. Some of Jesus' followers were used to catching fish. Now they would be catching people for God's kingdom.

What is the literary form? Is it narrative, telling a story? Is it poetic, like the book of Psalms or Job? Is it a letter, like many of the books in the New Testament? Is it prophetic, like Daniel and many of the books in the Old Testament? Or is it didactic, meaning "designed or intended to teach," like Jesus' Sermon on the

Mount? In this case, the passage is a narrative. Mark is recounting a story, vividly told, so that his readers will easily understand. His style is swift, as if he wants to plant as many visual images as possible, yet keep the story moving along.

2. WHEN? *When do these events take place?* According to the text, it was at the "beginning of the gospel of Jesus Christ." Mark is showing how the ministry of Jesus Christ began, according to the prophecy of Isaiah, with a forerunner named John, who announced the imminent arrival of Jesus. There was a baptism at this same time, and then notice the timing of the following events: "Immediately the Spirit drove Him into the wilderness." The wording is obviously designed to show that there was no time wasted. It wasn't *eventually*, but *immediately*. God had a timetable to keep and that included baptism as well as temptation. We also notice the exact time when Jesus began proclaiming His message. It was "after John was put in prison." All these observations help us to see that when John's voice was silenced, the Messiah's voice was heard. Uncovering these interesting facts adds to our enjoyment and understanding of the Bible.

3. WHERE? *Where did these incidents take place?* What is the geographical setting? The scene opens at the Jordan River, shifts to the wilderness of Judea, and ends at the Sea of Galilee. A lot of territory is covered in just twenty verses.

Where did all these people come from? They came from the land of Judea and the city of Jerusalem to be baptized. *Where* did Jesus and John go in the story? Jesus went into the wilderness for forty days and John went to prison. These are the kinds of first impressions and general observations we can make by asking questions about a section or verse. It may prove helpful to look up geographical locations in a Bible dictionary or find them on the maps in the back of your Bible. The knowledge you'll glean about topography, distances, population base, and terrain changes will add to the intrigue of the story.

4. HOW? *How does Mark's account contribute to the story of Jesus Christ?* This may be harder to discover, but a little patience and keen observation will help to make your exercise more interesting. The word "immediately" is used several times. This pattern is peculiar to Mark. Notice that he begins many of his sentences with words such as *then* and *now*. These words give his narrative a sense of immediacy, of constant, progressive action. By noticing these subtleties, we get the notion that Mark is portraying Jesus as a servant who is always on the go, always concerned about doing the will of His Father in heaven, always keeping in sync with the heavenly timetable.

How did John conduct his ministry? He followed and fulfilled the Scriptures with humility and then phased out completely after Christ came on the scene.

How did Jesus pick His disciples? He chose them from a low-caste occupation and conferred on them an extremely high calling. He called them with the simple directive, "Follow me."

5. WHO? *Who is involved in this passage?* There were lots of people: John the Baptist, Jesus, Simon, Andrew, Satan, some angels, God the Father, and the Holy Spirit. We also have James, John, and their father, Zebedee. There were also crowds of people from the environs of Jerusalem and other towns of Judea. If we were to investigate the identity of each person and his reason for being included in this passage, it would take us further along the path of observation. We see that, from the beginning, the ministry of Jesus included many people. That's a key element in the Gospels. Though we sometimes find Jesus alone with His Father in prayer, getting spiritually recharged, He came to touch people's lives, and the lives He touched were those of the common people—including fishermen. *Who chose the disciples?* Even though many interested people surrounded Jesus, he selected specific individuals to be His disciples.

6. WHY? We can apply this question several ways. *Why did God send John?* According to the text quoted from the prophet Isaiah, it was to "prepare the way" for Jesus. John's work as the lone voice "crying in the wilderness" created enough attention that people came from everywhere to find out about the coming Messiah.

Why did Jesus leave Nazareth? He left to go south to the Jordan River to be baptized, then into the wilderness to be tempted, and then to Galilee to preach to the people and call His disciples.

Why did Simon, Andrew, James, and John leave their fishing business? Jesus' authoritative call and claim on their lives provided enough impetus and excitement that a radical change was in order.

Why did Mark write this account? Are there any clues here? We would need to read the entire Gospel to answer this question, but there are hints in this passage. In the first verse, Mark begins with a declaration of faith that Jesus Christ is the Son of God. He wants us to know that he believes Jesus to be the promised Messiah, the One who is also God's Son. Throughout the book, he makes mention of the reaction of the people to Jesus: They were astonished at Him. It seems obvious that he wrote this account to help us discover what those who saw and heard Him had already discovered: Jesus was no ordinary man. Jesus wasn't just a good man. He was the God-man, and life has no higher reward than following Him.

You can see that by asking investigative questions, we gain insight into what the Holy Spirit was trying to convey through the original authors of the Bible. This is part of the illumination process—the Spirit of God revealing the Word of God to the people of God. You can also experience the joy of discovery as you uncover for yourself what God has revealed in His Word. It's one of the most pleasurable endeavors you'll ever undertake. Nothing else can quite compare!

OBSERVATION LEVEL THREE: DIGGING DEEPER

After our "flyover" and "ground-level" studies, there's yet another level of inquiry where we dig beneath the surface to uncover insights and details that are not as readily apparent as the information we have gathered thus far. We could call this a "worm's-eye" view. With each successive stage, we draw closer to the author's original intent and deepen our understanding of God's truth. Also, by stimulating our minds to observe and gather information, we stimulate our hearts toward spiritual transformation.

Digging deeper involves six focus points for our observations:

1. Repeated Words and Phrases
2. Peculiar Words and Phrases
3. Comparisons and Contrasts
4. Figurative Expressions
5. Anything Strange
6. Picturing Yourself in the Scene

Observe Repeated Words and Phrases

Certain structural and stylistic patterns can help us understand the author's meaning and emphasis. It may be beneficial for you to circle these words or phrases to be able to analyze them later and find out their overall relation to the text. In the first twenty verses of the Gospel of Mark, we see that the words *gospel* and *preaching* are repeated three times each. The word *gospel* refers to good news, and "to preach" means to "herald or proclaim something, to state it plainly and definitely." In this context, John the Baptist was heralding and proclaiming the good news of Jesus Christ. After John was silenced, Jesus also started preaching. The front-runner picked up where the forerunner left off. This important observation shows a continuity of purpose. Later, at the end of the book, the followers of Jesus will do the same—they will be told by Jesus himself to announce the good news of salvation to the whole world.

We have already discussed that the repeated use of the word *immediately* is a key to the Gospel of Mark. This stylistic element of Mark's authorship depicts the flow and intensity of the life of

Jesus. In almost every passage of Scripture you study there will be repeated words and phrases. Train yourself to notice them.

Observe Peculiar Words and Phrases

As you read, you'll notice occasional words that seem unusual or that we don't use on an everyday basis. Some of these words may be keys to understanding the meaning of the text. They may be words that made sense in the context of ancient Jewish culture but don't translate well into our postmodern society. For example, in the verses at hand, the word *repentance* might stand out as unusual. For many, it might conjure up images of sackcloth and ashes, fasting, or taking long, barefoot walks in the desert in the searing heat. Here's where a Bible dictionary comes in handy. If we look up the word *repentance*, we find a summary of how the word is used in the Old and New Testaments, as well as an explanation of the original Hebrew and Greek words. Here's a portion of the definition found in the *New Bible Dictionary*:

> The term used most frequently [in the Old Testament] to denote human repentance . . . means to turn or return and is applied to turning from sin to God. . . . In the New Testament, the terms 'repent' . . . and 'repentance' . . . refer basically to a change of mind. . . . Repentance consists in a radical transformation of thought, attitude, outlook, and direction.[1]

That clears some fog from the subject, doesn't it? "Repentance" is an active word involving both the heart and outward actions. The basic idea is to turn around. It implies more than just "being sorry" about something. It means to change one's mind and change one's actions accordingly. As you notice peculiar words—or even just words you don't understand—get in the habit of looking them up to accurately understand their meaning.

Our text in Mark also includes a peculiar phrase: "the remission of sins." Some newer translations substitute an equivalent rendering, such as "forgiveness of sins" or "release from sins." You might find a definition in a Bible dictionary, in the margin of your Bible, or as a footnote. Often words like these can be found in an English dictionary as well—including the original root meaning. In *Merriam-Webster's Collegiate Dictionary*, tenth edition, *remission* is defined as "the act or process of remitting" (don't you love those clear definitions?), which means, in part, "to release from the guilt or penalty of" or "to cancel or refrain from inflicting."

By studying the definitions of these two "peculiar" words, we have not only gained insight into some fundamental concepts of salvation, we have also explained why John the Baptist preached and why Jesus came into the world. They came to deal with the sin problem that has plagued humanity from the beginning. I don't know about you, but I enjoy discovering how all these individual threads are woven together in the tapestry of Scripture.

Observe Comparisons and Contrasts

To see one thing more clearly, it often helps to compare it to something else. For example, we gain a new appreciation for the wonders of our laptop or desktop computers when we compare them to the first computers from the 1940s, which were the size of an eighteen-wheel tractor-trailer rig and weighed more than seventeen Chevrolet Camaros. John the Baptist paints a compelling contrast when he compares himself, as God's messenger, to the coming Messiah, of whom he says, "There comes One after me who is mightier than I, whose sandal strap I am not worthy to stoop down and loose." And then, with that picture in mind, he compares the impact of his ministry with that of Jesus Christ: "I indeed baptized you with water, but He will baptize you with the Holy Spirit."

Another interesting contrast in this passage is the difference between John's wilderness experience and that of Jesus. John, we're told, "came baptizing in the wilderness and preaching a baptism of repentance for the remission of sins. . . . [He] was clothed with camel's hair and with a leather belt around his waist, and he ate locusts and wild honey." When Jesus was driven into the wilderness by the Holy Spirit, "He was there . . . forty days, tempted by Satan, . . . and the angels ministered to Him." In a few short phrases, we see a contrast between John's life of preaching and baptizing and living off the land and Jesus' mission of confronting the principalities of evil with supernatural assistance by the angels. In this depiction of the courier of evil tempting Jesus while the couriers of grace were serving Him, we see the conflict between heavenly forces that was central to the work of Jesus.

Observe Figurative Expressions

Figures of speech are phrases that add spice and flavor to our communication. We use such idiomatic expressions all the time in everyday speech, and virtually every language has them. For example, we might say, "His argument *doesn't hold water*." This is a figurative way of conveying doubt in someone's reasoning process. Sometimes we'll hear people say they are *standing on God's Word*. Does that mean there's a Bible under their feet? No. They are simply affirming, in a colorful way, their reliance on what God has said in the Bible. The Bible itself contains many examples of figurative speech. Our text in Mark has a few that are obvious:

"And he preached, saying, "There comes One after me who is mightier than I, whose sandal strap I am not worthy to stoop down and loose" (Mark 1:7). A good Bible dictionary would shed some light on what John is saying. In the ancient near east, when a guest entered the house, a servant would stoop to untie his sandals as a gesture of hospitality. So John is figuratively saying that he is not even worthy to be Jesus' servant. In comparison to the exalted place of the Messiah, even the lowest place in the house would be too high for John to occupy.

"Then Jesus said to them, 'Follow Me, and I will make you become fishers of men' " (Mark 1:17). Did Jesus mean that the disciples would literally throw their fishing nets over people in order to preach to them? Obviously not. He was simply using a metaphor that a group of rough-hewn fishermen could understand. When they chose to follow Jesus, they would figuratively cast their nets to draw other people to God. In a sense, Jesus elevated their view of their occupation and gave them a higher calling—catching the souls of men and women.

Another figurative device is the use of exaggeration to make a point. Mark records that "all the land of Judea, and those from Jerusalem, went out to him and were all baptized" (Mark 1:5). What he means is that people were streaming out to John from everywhere in that region, even from the headquarters of the Jewish religion—Jerusalem. This wasn't an occasional dunking—multitudes were being baptized!

Observe Anything Strange

As you read your Bible, you'll notice many strange things. In fact, it can be a lot of fun. Consider John the Baptist, for example. Notice anything strange about him? What's *not* strange, right? When was the last time you saw someone come to church wearing a camel-hair tunic cinched with a leather belt? If someone did, how far down the aisle would he get? And how often do you meet someone who lives out in the desert and eats locusts? When we identify these "strange things" in a passage, they often help us focus on unique events and truths. John's dress was primitive and coarse to show the people that he wasn't doing his job for comfort and prestige. Perhaps it would remind them of Elijah the prophet, who also wore simple, sturdy clothing (2 Kings 1:8).

The place where these events took place was also strange. Looking at a Bible atlas or map, we can see that the Jordan River wasn't exactly the epicenter of the civilized world. In fact, it was precisely the opposite. Even though the center of Judaism was in Jerusalem, John brought his message of repentance to a dry, dusty, and virtually forsaken area about thirty miles away. Why did he baptize people there rather than at one of the populated pools in

Jerusalem, such as Bethesda or Siloam? In town, folks could have walked a few yards to be baptized—or a couple of miles at the most. But with John down at the Jordan River, people had to hear by word of mouth and then trek out into the middle of nowhere to be baptized. We know that it had been prophesied that John would be a voice crying in the wilderness, but why? Was it to detach the people from their religious surroundings so they would focus on life's essentials? Was it to demonstrate that we don't need the trappings of a religious system to have a relationship with God? Are these important questions? We really don't know until we dig deeper. Careful observation will teach us to look for these kinds of things—the fun challenges we encounter in personal Bible study.

Observe by Picturing Yourself in the Scene

A technique that has helped me over the years in studying the Scriptures is picturing myself in the scene. When I step into the story, I begin to see things more from the author's perspective:

> On a hot afternoon in the Judean countryside, I'm traveling to Jerusalem, wearing a simple tunic and open-toed sandals. As I near the Jordan River, I suddenly come upon a crowd that is making its way down toward the water. The dust from their feet rises in a long trail toward the horizon. There are hundreds, perhaps thousands, of people walking out into the wilderness! I follow along and when I get to the river, I'm shocked! The stench of thousands of sweaty bodies huddled in the stark noontime sun is arresting. But they seem mesmer-

> ized. Here, in the middle of nowhere, surrounded by only dirt, rocks, and shimmering heat, they are listening to a sermon! The preacher speaks in a loud voice, calling people to repentance. When he is through, a throng of people rush forward, splashing their way into the water and asking the preacher to perform an ancient ritual usually reserved for those going up to Jerusalem's holy temple. Suddenly, the crowd recedes a bit, making room for a lone man whom the preacher seems to recognize. After a brief conversation with the preacher, he too is baptized. When he comes out of the water, the cloudless sky rumbles for a few seconds. The man looks up as if someone has just spoken to him.

Now you try it. Picture yourself in the midst of a crowd gathered in a remote, desert area. As you imagine this dramatic scene, you'll notice something else you may have never noticed before: The leather-bound book that you carry back and forth to church has started to come alive. Your understanding is being deepened, your perception heightened. You're enjoying yourself! The Bible has become interesting, stimulating, and enjoyable to read.

Every spring, the butterflies and bees descend on blossoming meadows, seeking nourishment from the fresh flowers. The butterfly darts here and there, sipping only the external sweets. He alights but for a second and then quickly moves on his fluttering way. The bee, however, goes deeper. Even if the flower is closed, the industrious little insect is not deterred. He pushes and penetrates his way in until he finds the hidden, luscious nectar. The bee comes to the flower empty, but he always leaves full! In your study of God's Word, dive and dig until you've tasted every last drop of spiritual nectar and are satisfied by its sweetness.

I love the way A. B. Simpson put Bible study in perspective when he wrote the following insight:

> God has hidden every precious thing in such a way that it is a reward to the diligent, a prize to the earnest, but a disappointment to the slothful soul. All nature is arrayed against the lounger and the idler. The nut is hidden in its thorny case; the pearl is buried beneath the ocean waves; the gold is imprisoned in the rocky bosom of the mountains; the gem is found only after you crush the rock which encloses it; the very soil gives its harvest as a reward to the laboring farmer. So truth and God must be earnestly sought.

"Cut your own wood and you warm yourself twice," Henry Ford reportedly said. He meant that the man who chops his own firewood not only enjoys the heat from the logs burning in his fireplace, but he also gets physically warmed from the exercise involved in his labor. Diligent study of God's Word will warm the soul like nothing else can. It will keep the flame of devotion alive as well as fuel your mind to learn more about God.

---

[1]J. D. Douglas, ed., *The New Bible Dictionary* (Grand Rapids, Mich.: Eerdmans, 1962).

5

INTERPRETATION: OPENING YOUR MIND

It is always easier to understand what the Bible says than to understand what somebody thinks it meant to say. —VANCE HAVNER

"WELL, THAT'S *your* interpretation." Have you ever heard this retort when you tried to share a truth from Scripture? It might make you stop and wonder: *Are they right? Maybe my understanding of the Bible is way off track.* If it's possible to derive more than one interpretation from the same passage of Scripture, how can we be certain that our perspective is correct? Certainly, beneath the large umbrella of Christianity, there are disagreements about specific passages of Scripture or doctrines, such as the precise chronology of the return of Jesus Christ, the application of certain spiritual gifts within the contemporary church, the issue of man's free will versus God's sovereignty, the controversy over eternal security, and many others. However, when it comes to the *essentials* of the Christian faith, such as the Person and work of Jesus Christ, His deity, His atoning death on the cross and subsequent resurrection, and the *fact* of His impending return, there is unity among believers. From the time the church was established, it has been bound together by these essential, orthodox (accepted as standard) beliefs.

In our study of Scripture, we want to understand the truth objectively, independent of preconceived notions, rather than simply leaning toward our own biases. Otherwise, we risk ending up like the driver of a tour bus in Nashville, Tennessee, who was pointing out sites from the Civil War battle of Nashville. "Right over here," he said, "a small group of Confederate soldiers held off a whole Yankee brigade." A little farther along, he said, "Over there, a young Confederate boy held off a Yankee platoon all by himself." This went on and on until finally a member of the tour group asked, "Didn't the North win anything in the battle of Nashville?" The bus driver replied, "Not while I'm the driver of this bus, they didn't!"

Whenever we look for the interpretation of a passage, our purpose is simply to find out what the author originally intended the hearers or readers to understand. In the previous chapter, we learned that *observation* means to open our eyes to what the text is saying by getting an overall perspective, asking pertinent questions, and taking notes. In this chapter we will learn about opening our minds to the meaning of those observations. Don't worry! Interpretation doesn't have to be an intimidating process. In fact, it will add to the enjoyment of our discoveries. What we have *observed* has laid a foundation of facts on which we can now build our understanding.

Maybe you're thinking, *This isn't all that important. As long as I read my Bible and listen to what my pastor or the preacher on TV says, I'll be fine.* Wrong! In fact you may end up so confused that you won't know which end is up. Just because someone stands in front of a microphone or a camera doesn't mean he is saying all the right things. Consider this sober warning from Dave Hunt and T. A. McMahon in their fine book *The Seduction of Christianity:*

> Christianity may well be facing the greatest challenge in its history: A series of powerful and growing seductions that are subtly changing biblical interpretations and undermining the faith of millions of people. Most Christians are scarcely aware of what is happening, and much less do they understand the issues involved.
>
> The seduction is surprisingly easy. It does not take place as an obvious frontal assault from rival religious beliefs. That would be vigorously resisted. Instead, it comes to some Christians in the guise of faith-producing techniques for gaining spiritual power and experiencing miracles and to others as self-improvement psychologies for fully realizing human potential that are seen as scientific aids to successful Christian living.[1]

When it comes to the Word of God, we cannot afford to be passive. If we learn how to interpret the Scriptures for ourselves, we will boost our discernment and deepen our understanding. It takes a personal knowledge of the Scriptures to ward off these subtle attacks. Proper interpretation is essential in studying God's revelation. The Bible tells us to "be diligent to present yourself approved to God as a workman who does not need to be ashamed, handling accurately the word of truth" (2 Timothy 2:15, NASB). If we develop a good plan of analysis that follows certain rules of interpretation, we can evaluate the observations we've made and be reasonably certain that we will arrive at an accurate interpretation.

SHEDDING LIGHT ON INTERPRETATION

In our discussion of "observation" (chapter 4), we considered six basic questions that we should ask about each passage of Scripture that we study. In the "interpretation" step, there are five questions that will help us grasp the meaning and intent of what we've read:

1. What is the context?
2. What do the words mean?
3. What does the grammar show?
4. What is the background?
5. How does your interpretation balance with the rest of Scripture?

What Is the Context?

The first thing to do when evaluating a portion of Scripture is to look at the surrounding verses, which provide the context—the connective fiber—for the passage we are studying. When forensic investigators examine a crime scene, they observe not only the body itself but the entire scene—the surrounding elements that may lead to a discovery of what exactly happened. In the same way, when it comes to "investigating" a passage of Scripture, we should look at what comes before and after the passage. A good practice is to trace the "thread of thought" wherever it might run. To do this, find where the author introduces the thought and track it to its conclusion. We may find that many passages have an entirely different meaning *in context* than when isolated from it. If we ignore context, we can make the Bible say almost anything we choose. For example, if we wanted to build a case for the non-existence of God, we could extract the following quote from Psalm 53:1: "There is no God." But when we consider the entire verse, the meaning becomes plain: "The fool has said in his heart, 'There is no God.'" When the phrase is seen in the context of the entire verse, it means the *exact opposite* of our initial interpretation. Granted, this is a simplistic example, but the principle is the same whether it's a word, phrase, or paragraph. The true meaning of a verse is the one provided by its context. Most false doctrines and aberrant teachings arise from neglecting this principle. To put it another way, *any text without a context becomes a pretext*.

There are two levels of context to keep in mind—*immediate* and *remote*. Immediate context refers to the sentence in which a word is found or the paragraph in which a sentence is found. Remote context refers to the entire progression of thought leading up to the verse. Let's take a look at a familiar passage to get a feel for this:

> Therefore we also, since we are surrounded by so great a cloud of witnesses, let us lay aside every weight, and the sin which so easily ensnares us, and let us run with endurance the race that is set before us, looking unto Jesus, the author and finisher of our faith, who for the joy that was set before Him endured the cross, despising the shame, and has sat down at the right hand of the throne of God. (HEBREWS 12:1-2)

The immediate context is found here in the first two verses of chapter 12, which refer to a race of faith that is to be run with endurance. The author speaks of how to run that race and who to keep our eyes on while we run. The remote context, on the other hand, is suggested by the first word of chapter 12, "therefore," which draws our attention back to chapter 11. There we find several examples of faith as portrayed by various saints down through the ages. The word *therefore* informs us that what is said in chapter 12 is "as a result of" what has been revealed in chapter 11. In that context, then, we know that the "cloud of witnesses" refers to the list of faithful people in chapter 11. The passage is couched in terms of an athletic event, which was a common point of reference in ancient Greece and Rome. The faithful saints of old are presented as "witnesses" to our present "race." Warm-up weights are representative of sin, which is to be laid aside in the serious competition of life. In its context, the verse is saying that the life of faith is like a race in which we are required to "run with endurance," just as others have successfully run before us.

What Do the Words Mean?

Just about every human society uses words as the primary vehicle of communication. Our ability to articulate in language distinguishes us from other living creatures. There is no parallel to human speech in the animal world. Conversation is uniquely human. In fact, on average we spend about one-fifth of our lives talking. Each of us will use enough words in a lifetime to fill a library of three thousand large volumes totaling approximately 1.5 million words!

Because the Bible, like any book, was written by stringing words together to form coherent thoughts, we form our interpretations based on the words used. This seems obvious and easy enough; however, there are some problems. For example, some words have more than one meaning. If I say "light," you may not know exactly what I mean. Am I referring to the electromagnetic waves emanating from the sun? Do I mean the opposite of heavy? Perhaps I am trying to describe the shade of a color. Other words (context) would be required to form a solid understanding. A dictionary may also be helpful in order to get a firm grasp on precisely what the word conveys. The Bible uses "light" in much the same manner. It may refer to the light of the sun, as in Genesis 1:3 when God said, "'Let there be light'; and there was light." Or it may carry a figurative connotation, as in the words of Simeon when he saw the Christ child and declared Him to be "a light to bring revelation to the Gentiles, and the glory of Your people Israel" (Luke 2:32). *Light* could also mean "to deem something as unimportant." Jesus used it this way when He told the parable of the wedding feast and described the response of those who refused to come by saying, "But they made light of it and went their ways, one to his own farm, another to his business" (Matthew 22:5). Usually the context will clear things up in such cases.

As we translate or interpret specific words, we must remember that language is fluid. Words and meanings change over time. In the old days, for example, the word *conversation* meant something entirely different than it does today. The King James translation of Hebrews 13:5 says, "Let your conversation be without covetousness," which makes it sound like we shouldn't reveal our base desires when we speak. But that is not the meaning of the verse. A more modern rendering would be, "Let your conduct be without covetousness." Why the change? Simply because the meaning of the English word *conversation* has changed. Once upon a time, it meant "conduct" or "one's manner of life." Over time, the meaning changed until now conversation refers to "talk," not action.

To understand the words used in a passage, we must first observe how they fit into the context. Then, looking up some of them in the dictionary to see if they have more than one meaning will help us nail down the precise meaning. Some words can be found in a Bible dictionary, which will explain their specific meanings in the Old and New Testaments. One good resource is W. E. Vine's *Expository Dictionary of Biblical Words*.

What Does the Grammar Show?

I know, I know. Right about now you're saying, "I thought the title of this book said something about *enjoying* Bible study—and now he's talking about grammar? I'm outta here!" Hold on. I'm not trying to conjure up images of your high school English class. I'm simply trying to help you *understand* what you read, because therein lies the enjoyment! Words are always used in combination with other words. The relationship of those words provides the meaning. What can you tell about a person who shouts out, "Nuts!"? Did he hurt himself? Did he forget something? Did he find some acorns on the trail while walking in the woods? We need other words to make the meaning clear. The other words will have a certain function in the sentence that unravels the role of the word we're considering. To understand what a person means when he writes or speaks, both parties must have the same understanding of how words relate to one another in the sentences or paragraph. Don't be afraid of words; use them to your advantage.

You don't have to be an English major to understand the Bible. It helps, however, to identify the parts of speech: noun, pronoun, verb, adverb, preposition, conjunction, and so on. Another thing to look for is how these words relate in the sentence.

After the resurrection, Jesus asked Peter, "Simon, son of Jonah, do you love Me more than these?" (John 21:15). What did Jesus mean? Did Peter love Him more than what—more than whom? The dictionary reveals that "these" is an adjective or a demonstrative pronoun, "being the person, thing, or idea that is present or near in place, time, or thought, or that has just been mentioned." Well then, what person, thing, or idea was present or had just been mentioned? In the story, the disciples had just been fishing and had caught some fish. Perhaps Jesus was referring to Peter's love for catching fish and was therefore asking him about his priorities, as if to say, "Peter, am I more important than your occupation?"

"These" could also mean "these other disciples." After all, it was Peter who had earlier boasted that he was more faithful than everyone else. When Jesus predicted that they would all stumble when He was crucified, Peter piped up, "Even if all are made to stumble because of You, I will never be made to stumble" (Matthew 26:33). That was quite a claim. Maybe Jesus was reminding Peter of his previous boast now that His travail and death were over. Can you see how grammar can help you understand the meaning? It may not always be able to convey the exact and undisputed meaning, but it can show you the viable alternatives.

When looking at a passage of Scripture, give some attention to the structure. Try to identify the key thought of the verse by first finding the subject (the main thing or person) and verb (the action or condition of the subject.) Then notice the relationship of the other words around it. Try to come up with all the possible meanings. If you see more than one, consider the word in light of the context.

What Is the Background?

Have you ever walked in late to a play or a movie? Frustrating, isn't it? The plot has already begun to unfold, the key characters have been introduced, and the setting has been revealed. So, by the time you find your seat, you're confused and frustrated because you've missed out on some important information—the background! You wonder, *Who's that character talking about? Why did he say that? What does he mean by that?* Then you frustrate others who have been watching from the beginning by pestering them with questions while they're trying to enjoy the show!

Reading a single paragraph or even a chapter in the Bible can produce the same effect. We often jump right into the middle of a story and neglect to discover the setting, the plot, and key characters. We lift out a text and memorize it without considering the background, cultural customs, or historical setting. When we do this, we can fall into the trap of interpreting the passage in the context of our own culture and setting. That's fine when it comes to application of the Bible, but in order to come to an accurate interpretation, we first must see the Bible in its original setting and background.

Have you ever stopped to consider that the Bible has a setting? The events took place within a certain culture—a Middle Eastern Semitic culture. The societies were mostly agrarian and simple. The cities were small and compact and had towers, walls, and gates for protection. They generally were on elevated sites with a water source nearby for sustenance and protection. Water didn't come from the tap but was fetched from huge cisterns or wells. The clothing was certainly different. Rather than being purchased from a mall, it was handmade, earthy, and simple. The basic article of clothing was the tunic, to which various accessories were added. Understanding the lifestyle, customs, and language of the day helps us interpret the setting and meaning of the Bible.

Why is this important? Simply because there were customs and expressions in ancient biblical cultures with which we are totally unfamiliar. An idiom that had meaning in one culture or at one time in history doesn't necessarily have the same meaning in another. Ask any missionary about this. Leaving the comforts of home and going abroad to another culture can be very disorienting. The language is different. So are the customs and the weather, not to mention the food! Once, while visiting the Philippines, I was served funny-tasting meat that I courageously consumed in order to prove that I could acclimate to any culture. I'll admit, the taste was a bit exotic, but I wasn't going to be deterred. It wasn't until a couple of days later that one of the locals told me I had consumed a fat, juicy wormburger!

When we turn to the pages of Scripture, we find similar cultural gaps that must be noted and understood. For example, when we read of the man who wanted first to go "bury his father" before he would follow Jesus, we might be a bit put off by Jesus' terse response. He told this young man, "Follow Me, and let the dead bury their own dead." What? How insensitive can Jesus be? After all, this guy just lost his dad, right? Not necessarily.

A few years ago, a missionary asked a rich young Turkish man to go with him on a trip to Europe, during which time the missionary hoped to disciple the man. When the young man replied that he must bury his father, the missionary offered his sympathy and expressed surprise that the father had died. The man told him that his father was alive and healthy. He explained that the expression "bury my father" meant staying at home and fulfilling his family responsibilities until his father died and he received his share of the inheritance. So, what the man who came to Jesus was saying was equivalent to, "I want to wait until I receive my inheritance." Well, that could involve a long period of time—many years if the father was still young and in good health.

Another example of the importance of background is found in John 13 when Jesus washed the disciples' feet at the Last Supper. He then told them to do the same to others. Does this mean that Christians ought to pull the socks off other Christians and scrub away? The background of the culture gives us a clue. Before meals were eaten, the hands were always washed under running water, because there were no utensils such as knives, forks, and spoons. Under certain conditions, guests who had just come into the house after walking the dusty or even muddy Middle Eastern roads would have their feet washed. In a wealthy home, a servant would perform this task. By New Testament times, foot washing had become something of a ritual.

In context, then, Jesus was taking on the role of a servant by washing the feet of the disciples at the Last Supper. He was telling His followers to be willing to take the lowest place among others—that of a servant. Jesus explains the meaning of his actions in this scene, but the full significance might not register with us unless we're familiar with the ancient custom of foot washing. The same principle holds true today in many cultures. As the Bible is translated into various languages and brought into different cultural settings, idioms are taken into consideration. One spokesman from the American Bible Society gave the following report: "We in the United States love the Lord with our 'heart,' but the Karre people of French Equatorial Africa love Him with their 'liver.' The Conob Indians of Guatemala love with their 'stomachs,' and the Marshall Islanders in the North Pacific, with their 'throats.'"

Do all these different words in the various languages distort the message? Not at all. In each tongue they are synonymous with the overall sense of the original. Although we say in English that "I press toward the goal" (Philippians 3:14), and the Navajo Indians say, "I run with my mouth open," it is one and the same truth.

Knowing the background, customs, and culture of the Bible will help us interpret and apply its true meaning to our lives. But how can we find out these things? First of all, we need to read the Bible regularly. The more we learn about the Scriptures as a whole, the more we'll understand about the culture. You might be surprised to find that a lot of the background information is right there in the Bible. The Old Testament is background for the New Testament, and certain books provide background for others. For example, the book of Leviticus will aid our understanding of the New Testament book of Hebrews. As a matter of fact, the author of Hebrews assumes his readers have a working knowledge of the Israelite sacrificial system. Much of the background for the letters of Paul can be found in the book of Acts, which records his journeys and experiences in the cities of Philippi, Ephesus, Thessalonica, and others.

Studying maps is another way to gain insight. The maps in the back of most Bibles are a good place to start, but atlases often provide more information and explanation. We can also look up cross-references printed in the margins of our Bible. These parallel verses often shed light on what we are reading. If we have some of the Bible study resources listed in chapter 2, such as a Bible dictionary or concordance, we can look up certain words that will enrich our study. Many commentaries will also shed cultural and historical light on the passage in question.

Perhaps the ultimate way to get a large dose of biblical background, though it may sound a bit expensive, is to go on a tour of Israel. It has been said that "to visualize is to empathize." Traveling the land itself and seeing where all the events took place is worth more than any stack of books. Seeing the layout, distances, topography, and climate of the "land of the Book" will enhance your understanding. Once you've walked where Jesus, Moses, and the prophets walked, you will never read your Bible the same way again.

How Does Your Interpretation Balance with the Rest of Scripture?

The term "balance" has become a modern evangelical watchword, and for good reason. It's easy to get off balance—even among Christians. We can emphasize one doctrine to the neglect of all the others. We can use a "proof text" to substantiate (albeit erroneously) almost anything in the world. We need to consider the "full counsel of Scripture" in arriving at any particular interpretation. In other words, the ultimate context of any text is the entire Bible. *Sola scriptura interpres*, one of the axioms developed during the

Reformation, still holds true. It simply means, "Scripture interprets Scripture." The importance of this principle can be readily understood when our interpretation of a specific portion of Scripture contradicts the *teaching of the Bible as a whole*. If such is the case, we'd better put on the interpretative brakes. The Bible doesn't contradict itself. Because it has basically one Author or Superintendent—the Holy Spirit—His message is consistent, cohesive, and coherent.

The Bible is really a fabulous document. Essentially it is a compilation of many books (sixty-six), written over a period of sixteen hundred years by more than forty authors from different social backgrounds, yet with a unified message. The prophet Amos was a shepherd; Daniel was a political leader; and Joshua was a general. In the New Testament, Peter and John were fishermen; Luke was a Gentile physician; Paul, the great missionary, was once a prominent Jewish rabbi. The Bible was written on three separate continents (Africa, Asia, and Europe) in three different languages (Hebrew, Aramaic, and Greek). It deals with controversial subjects such as the origin of the universe, the existence of God, the origin and ultimate end of evil, and the purpose of life. With such variables, one would expect a chaotic text, but we discover that the Bible reads as one grand, unfolding plan of redemption. Amos, Luke, Daniel, Joshua, and Paul all agree. That's unity!

Think of a comparable example. Imagine taking twenty-five medical books from various cultures, written in different languages over the past one thousand years, and trying to treat someone based on the findings. What do you think would happen to the patient? He'd probably be dead in a week—or less! Yet the Bible's diagnosis and prescription for the ills of humanity reads with synthesis and cohesion. Since its earliest days, it has successfully treated our sinful condition. That's why, when we interpret a specific passage, we must balance our findings with the rest of the Bible's teaching.

I mentioned previously that most cults have gone astray because someone, usually the leader, took verses out of context. In the same way, false teachings have crept into the church simply because certain passages have been emphasized while others are ignored. This can easily occur when the balance of truth is tampered with or ignored. We can keep ourselves from these kinds of errors by checking our understanding of a verse against the rest of the Bible. Don't isolate one section when forming a doctrinal position. For example, if we considered only Old Testament regulations pertaining to the Sabbath and dietary restrictions, without the balance of New Testament teaching, we might wind up as vegetable-eating Sabbatarians. The balance between the New Covenant and the Old Covenant, and the practices of the early church, help to temper our understanding and application. That's why we need to read all the way through the Bible and why our pastors need to teach through the whole Bible. A little appetizer from the Gospels and a midnight snack on the Psalms won't cut it. Neither will a smorgasbord of favorite texts. God gave us the full meal, and we need to feast on it.

In the Gospels (the accounts of Jesus' life and ministry written by Matthew, Mark, Luke, and John), one simple way to apply this principle is to look at parallel passages—those verses from each book that discuss the same event. Read, for instance, the miracle of the feeding of the five thousand (which appears in Matthew 14:13-21; Mark 6:33-44; Luke 9:12-17; and John 6:1-14). Notice how each author wrote with a different purpose in mind—so as to emphasize a particular aspect of who Jesus is. Seeing these accounts side by side broadens our understanding of what happened. In the Old Testament, if you're reading the historical accounts in the books of 1 and 2 Samuel and 1 and 2 Kings, look for parallel accounts of the same events in 1 and 2 Chronicles.

If all this talk of interpretation and critical thinking sounds a bit laborious, take heart! Just think of the payoff—the enjoyment of discovering and understanding God's truth. As you train your mind to ponder these truths, you will extract the life-giving nectar that will refresh and restore your soul.

M. A. Rosanoff, a longtime associate of Thomas Edison, worked steadily for more than a year trying to soften the wax of phonograph cylinders by altering their chemical constitution so that they would accept and preserve a recording of sound. Month after month, the results were negative. Rosanoff later recounted how he had mused night after night trying to "mentally cough up" every theoretical and practical solution. "Then it came like a flash of lightning," he said. "I could not shut waxes out of my mind, even in my sleep. Suddenly, through headache and daze, I was at my desk; and half an hour later I had a record in the softened wax cylinder. . . . This was the solution! I learned to think waxes . . . waxes . . . waxes, and the answer came without effort, although months of thought had gone into the mental mill."

Rosanoff's solution was to focus on the medium of "waxes" until he came up with the answer he was looking for. Similarly, God's Word will become clear to us when we meditate on it, muse over it, analyze it, and consider its context, language, background, and unity. As we immerse ourselves in Scripture and think Bible . . . Bible . . . Bible, we'll soon find that its truths are recorded in our changed lives.

---

[1] Dave Hunt and T. A. McMahon, *The Seduction of Christianity* (Eugene, Oreg.: Harvest House Publishers, 1985), 11.

6

GOD'S CREATIVE WRITING

If you wish to know God, you must know His Word. If you wish to perceive His power, you must see how He works by His Word. If you wish to know His purpose before it comes to pass, you can only discover it by His Word. —AUTHOR UNKNOWN

CREATIVITY IS THE GIFT of helping others see past the limitations of their natural eyes and see with their mind's eye. Creative communicators paint word pictures that help the reader or hearer to retain critical information. The more vivid the image, and the more senses the creator can involve, the more lasting the retention. That's one of the great things about the Bible. God is the consummate creative communicator!

The Bible was not written as a systematic theology text. Nor was it written as propositional theology. The Bible's subtitle is not "The doctrine of God, including theistic arguments for His existence." If it were, most of us would probably use the Bible as a cure for insomnia. Instead, our creative God wrote the Bible in a creative way. He appeals to our senses so that His truth can be enjoyed and retained.

A lot of Scripture is written in the form of a narrative—and it's no wonder. Everyone loves a good story. Stories reach out and engage the imagination. They draw us in and elicit a response as they stir up our feelings. Stories touch us in ways that lectures and seminars never will. Have you ever noticed how a congregation responds when a pastor inserts an illustration into his sermon? It's like turning on a light inside a room full of moths—everyone perks up. In the Bible, the stories of David, Ruth, Esther, and countless others capture our attention, awaken our senses, and involve our will. These stories of heroism, faith, failure, and redemption add texture and color to our understanding of the solid underlying principles.

The Bible is also filled with poetry. In fact, an entire section of biblical literature, including Job, Psalms, Proverbs, Ecclesiastes, Song of Solomon, and the book of Lamentations, is known as the poetic books. That's quite a chunk of the Old Testament! These books portray the experiences of God's people through a variety of vivid images. Poets think and speak without the restrictions of didactic communication. Instead they draw their colors from the palette of figurative language, painting pictures for the mind's eye. Because so much of the Bible is poetic, the use of colorful images often spills over into its prose. Unless we learn to appreciate this creative mode of expression, we simply cannot fully understand the Bible.

Let's consider the use of figurative language and its impact on our understanding and enjoyment of the Bible. I hope you'll appreciate God's creative genius in weaving together a variety of writing styles in His book.

PARABLES: FICTION THAT CONVEYS A FACT

Parables have been defined as earthly stories that convey heavenly truths. This definition stuck in my mind, as parables themselves are meant to do. It's no secret that Jesus was fond of using these stories when He taught crowds of spiritually hungry people. Storytelling was the ancient equivalent of modern television. It engaged people's sense of imagination. A skillful rabbi could weave together a story in such a way that the truth was embedded permanently in the hearts of his audience. Perhaps that's why Jesus used parables so often. He wasn't usually speaking in the synagogue to people who were bound to remain until the end of the service. He often spoke to crowds who were free to walk away at any time. Therefore, He used stories to pique their interest, rouse their curiosity, and draw them into an understanding of spiritual truth.

Parables in Scripture are pretty easy to spot. Whenever Jesus used one, He usually made it clear by saying, "Hear a parable," or "The kingdom of heaven is like . . ." Teaching by means of parables is effective because it takes abstract truth and makes it concrete in a way that is powerful, interesting, and memorable. When truth is presented in the guise of a parable, it is much easier to internalize the moral and spiritual meaning and apply it to life.

Parables were not meant to give specific detail as much as to illustrate an underlying meaning. Some scholars pick the parables apart and assign a figurative meaning to every detail. In so doing, they run the risk of distorting the original intent of the story. Generally, parables focused on one teaching, a single theme, and a central point that Jesus wanted to convey.

A word of caution is in order here. We should be careful not to base our doctrinal propositions on a parable alone—unless Jesus Himself interpreted it, and unless other Scriptures confirm our understanding. In the story of the sower and the seed (Matthew 13), Jesus explained the parable in great detail, giving us grounds for adequate and thorough interpretation. He explained that the field represented the world, the seed is the Word of God, and the sower is the one who dispenses the gospel. He taught us that Satan will snatch away the truth from people who close their hearts. Because Jesus named such specific points and details in the story and told us what they represented, a doctrine could be built on the parable of the sower and the seed. However, in cases where Jesus didn't explain the meaning of a parable, we have no right to assume an interpretation that is not plain in the text, or to force a meaning just because it fits with our theology. That would be sloppy and irresponsible interpretation.

TYPOLOGY: SHADOWS OF THE FUTURE

When you look at your shadow on a sunny afternoon, it is often elongated and distorted. It's not you, of course, but it *is* an image of you. A shadow resembles reality, even though it lacks substance. In the same way, in Scripture we find shadowy types that depict substantial spiritual truths. Listen to Paul's explanation in Colossians: "So let no one judge you in food or in drink, or regarding a festival or a new moon or sabbaths, which are a shadow of things to come, but the substance is of Christ" (Colossians 2:16-17). These feast days, or holy days, were merely representative of future things. They formed a "prophetic shadow" or a prefigurement of the reality to be found in Jesus Christ. We also see in the Old Testament a foreshadowing of things to come in the New Testament or beyond. Consider the Old Testament tabernacle. We know what it looked like, we know how it was established, and we know why God placed it in the midst of the encampment of the children of Israel. However, in some respects, the tabernacle was also a foreshadowing of heaven. The writer of Hebrews, after explaining the ordinances of the tabernacle, tells us about this typology:

> But Christ came as High Priest of the good things to come, with the greater and more perfect tabernacle not made with hands, that is, not of this creation. Not with the blood of goats and calves, but with His own blood He entered the Most Holy Place once for all, having obtained eternal redemption. . . . Therefore it was necessary that the copies of the things in the heavens should be purified with [the blood of calves and goats], but the heavenly things themselves with better sacrifices than these. For Christ has not entered the holy places made with hands, which are copies of the true,

> but into heaven itself, now to appear in the presence of God for us. (HEBREWS 9:11-12, 23-24)

The physical tabernacle contained copies of the things in the heavens. They were but sketches, or outlines, of the realities of heaven itself. Christ did not go into an earthly Holy of Holies in the temple of Jerusalem. He went into the presence of God, the heavenly—real—Holy of Holies. With this typology in mind, it's fascinating to read John's account of his vision of heaven in the book of Revelation. He sees a very "tabernacle-like" environment: seven lampstands burning with flames; a glassy sea, reminiscent of the laver used by the priests to wash; and the brilliant throne of God surrounded by four creatures with spread wings, reminding us of the Ark of the Covenant with the wings of angels covering it. We can readily observe how the heavenly realities follow the shadowy pattern of the tabernacle but then greatly exceed it in glory.

There are many such types and shadows throughout Scripture, and they will delight any Christian who reads the Old Testament in light of the New Testament, and vice versa. For example, the brass serpent in the wilderness (see Numbers 21:9) was a type of Christ. How do we know? Jesus provided the interpretation Himself in John 3:14: "And as Moses lifted up the serpent in the wilderness, even so must the Son of Man be lifted up." The land of Canaan is a type of the victorious life we can have as Christians, just as the Sabbath represents ceasing from our own works and resting in Christ. How do we know? The writer of Hebrews

ells us in chapters 3 and 4. The Passover and deliverance from
:gypt are types of our deliverance from sin, which is a constant
heme throughout the Bible. How do we know? Paul explained
t to the Corinthians: "For indeed Christ, our Passover, was sacri-
iced for us" (1 Corinthians 5:7). Also, on the last evening before
His crucifixion, Jesus took His disciples to an upper room and
nfused an old ritual with new significance. He told them that
vhen they celebrated the Passover from that time forward, they
vere to do it in His memory. Jesus was showing them that the
Old Testament sacrifice of the lamb and application of its blood
on the doorpost was a foreshadowing of the sacrifice of Christ
on the cross. He was the Lamb of God who takes away the sin
of the world. These types and shadows helped the disciples see
how the Old Covenant and the New Covenant were inextricably
woven together.

A type may be described as a "nonverbal prediction." For example, an Old Testament person or event may illustrate some aspect of the future without specifically describing it. The writer would have had no way to anticipate the future fulfillment of the type, but when viewed through the lens of later revelation, the meaning becomes clear. When we combine these nonverbal predictions with the more explicit verbal prophecies, we can see the fingerprint of the Holy Spirit on the writing of Scripture.

A note of caution is in order, however. We cannot legitimately label something as a type unless the Bible itself reveals the connection. If we don't keep this principle in mind, we may find ourselves allegorizing and spiritualizing Scripture without warrant.

PROPHECY: A WINDOW ON ETERNITY

A pastor once boasted that he didn't preach about prophecy because, in his words, "Prophecy only distracts people from the present." An astute colleague deftly retorted, "Well, then, there's certainly a lot of distraction in the Scriptures!" It's true. In fact, about one-fourth of the Bible was prophetic when it was written. Many of these prophecies have been fulfilled, and some are still awaiting fulfillment. Because much of the Bible includes a prophetic element, one of the most exciting and rewarding studies for any Christian is the study of prophecy.

Prophecy is history written in advance, or as Friedrich von Schlegel, the German writer, critic, and philosopher, noted, "A historian is a prophet in reverse." In the Bible, God draws aside the veil of the future, through prophecy, to give us an indication of what His plans are for the human race and the universe as a whole. The prophets are God's spokesmen, proclaiming events before they occur.

Fulfilled prophecy is one of God's calling cards. Because He knows everything, when He predicts certain events, they happen! For example, God said to Abraham, "Your descendants will be in a foreign land four hundred years," and guess what? They were! Before Babylon even existed as a military threat, God predicted through the prophets that Israel would be taken captive by the Babylonians. They were. He said their captivity would last seventy years—and it did! He further disclosed that Babylon would be overthrown by a character named Cyrus—two hundred years before Cyrus was born. God is not confined by space and time;

therefore He is able to speak of things past and things to come. "Remember the former things of old, for I am God, and there is no other; I am God, and there is none like Me, declaring the end from the beginning, and from ancient times things that are not yet done, saying, 'My counsel shall stand, and I will do all My pleasure'" (Isaiah 46:9-10). Prophecy is one of many ways by which God reveals Himself to us, and these passages are some of the more important and fascinating portions of Scripture.

The study of prophecy is not a fruitless exercise. On the contrary, when properly interpreted, biblical prophecy provides a guideline for godly living, motivating Christians to a high standard of holiness. Nevertheless, it is true that some have abused this sacred trust. Using the Bible, they have made claims about events which turned out later to be erroneous.

Just prior to 1988, some groups announced that the alignment of biblical prophecies indicated that Jesus would return that year. Books were written and congregations were warned to get ready. Even though Jesus Himself clearly taught that no one knows the exact time of His return, these groups were certain that they were the exception. When the date they "prophetically" selected turned out to be just another day, they became the laughingstock of the secular media. Just because a preacher says it doesn't mean it's the truth.

In 1870, a clergyman visiting his friend, a college president, expressed his conviction that the Bible declared that nothing new could be invented. The educator disagreed. "Why, in fifty years I believe it may be possible for men to soar through the air like birds!"

The visiting bishop was shocked. "Flight is strictly reserved for the angels," he replied, "and I beg you not to repeat your suggestion lest you be guilty of blasphemy!" Ironically, the bishop was none other than Milton Wright, the father of Orville and Wilbur. Thirty years later, near the small town of Kitty Hawk, North Carolina, his sons made the first flight in a heavier-than-air machine—the forerunner of the many planes that now dot our skies.

We must not be deterred by well-meaning-but-wrong interpreters who have misused the Bible. Predictions made by man are always replete with errors. I once read a newspaper story by someone who had evaluated all of the prophecies made by mediums, horoscope writers, and other would-be prognosticators during one calendar year, covering everything from the economy to the presidency. Of the six hundred predictions made, only thirty were actually fulfilled. Not a great record, to say the least. Now compare those "wild guesses" with the 330 Old Testament prophecies concerning the first coming of Jesus Christ, given hundreds of years before His birth. Every one of them came true. Mathematicians have attempted to calculate the likelihood (from a human perspective, of course) of 330 separate prophecies being fulfilled by one person. They estimated the odds at $1:884^{90}$. That's one chance in 884 followed by ninety zeros! When God is involved, prophecy is a powerful tool that opens a window on eternity.

Unfulfilled Prophecies from the Old and New Testaments

What about prophecies that haven't yet come true? For example, predictions about the Kingdom Age, the Millennium, and the second coming of Jesus Christ—when will these occur? One of the purposes of prophecy is to encourage our obedience in the present age. Jesus Himself warned His followers about the future so that they would learn how to live in the present. The idea isn't so much that we should try to guess when these prophecies might be fulfilled, but to help us remain spiritually alert and prepared as we wait for Christ's return. We should always live with a readiness for his imminent return (see Luke 12:40).

Prophecy is also intended to give us hope. As I write these words, the World Trade Center lies in ruins in New York, the Pentagon is badly damaged, and news reports are filled with speculation about how the United States will respond to the violence that has struck in our midst. In these uncertain times it would be easy to succumb to fear and anxiety. But God's plan for the future provides hope and encouragement because we know that He ultimately will intervene in history to conquer evil.

Prophecy in Perspective

When reading biblical prophecy, we have the advantage of perspective that earlier generations lacked. We can look from the Old Testament to the New Testament and see the many prophetic fulfillments that have already taken place. In that, we understand even better than the prophets themselves how the plan will ultimately come together.

Imagine looking at a mountain range from a great distance. The mountains appear flat and one-dimensional, as though they were painted on cardboard and propped up from behind. However, as we draw closer, or fly over the mountains in an airplane, we see the peaks and valleys, the rugged rocks, and the trees. From this perspective, it becomes obvious that the mountains are not flat at all but deeply layered. It's the same with prophecy. When the prophets of the Old Testament looked to the future, they saw two peaks: the advent of Christ and the second coming of Christ. Because from their vantage point they couldn't see the valley in between, they often blended the two peaks together. They didn't realize that there would be a two thousand-year gap between the two events. They did not foresee the Church Age. The apostle Paul made this clear when he spoke of "the mystery of the church" not revealed in the Old Testament. Perspective is an important concept to keep in mind as we look at prophecy, especially in the Old Testament.

There is a lot of debate these days concerning when Jesus will return. I hope it's soon and believe it will be. Will it happen before the time of tribulation that Jesus predicted? I'm certain that it will. Of course, there are almost as many views on this subject as there are people. Many are just plain bewildered by it all. George Sweeting tells of a seminary student who was befuddled by his professor's explanation of the timing of the Rapture. After several minutes of trying to sort through the pre-trib, mid-trib, and post-trib viewpoints, he folded his arms, leaned back in his chair, and said, "I-A-K."

"What does that mean?" the professor asked him.

"It means, 'I–am–confused.'"

"Confused doesn't start with a *k*," the professor replied.

"You don't know how confused I am!"

I believe that the more we read God's Word, the more we'll see God's plan and realize that it doesn't include God's children going through the same judgment that the unbelieving world will experience. Rather than confusion, the study of prophecy will bring confidence and contentment in whatever comes our way by the will of God.

INTERPRETING FIGURATIVE LANGUAGE

The biblical authors laced their writings with such vivid images that our senses are invigorated. Through the beauty of narrative, poetry, allegory, prophecy, and parable, the truth is embedded permanently in the depths of our souls. But because these colorful renditions are open to misunderstanding, we need to have a few guidelines to govern our interpretation.

1. *Interpret the text literally unless there's a good reason not to.* Take the passage at face value unless it is clearly written in figurative language. For example, in Revelation 1:16, when the Lord appears, it says, "Out of His mouth went a sharp two-edged sword." I doubt that John intended for us to take this description literally. In light of the awe-inspiring magnitude of his vision, he was probably grasping for a figurative expression of what he saw. In fact, in Revelation 1:1, we are told that these are signs: "The Revelation of Jesus Christ which God gave Him to show His servants—things which must shortly take place. And He sent and *signified* it . . ." (emphasis mine). The word translated here as "signified" means "a revelation through symbols."

2. *Look for clues in the text to help interpret figurative language*. For example, in Genesis 37, the dreams of Joseph are clearly understood to be prophetic. The images have a specific prophetic application, which the text discloses.

3. *If it's a figure of speech, interpret it figuratively*. Be aware of metaphors, which describe one thing in terms of something else, and similes, which compare one thing to another, usually preceded by the words *like* or *as*. And when you come across a phrase like, "He spoke a parable, saying . . . ," you know that an earthly story with a heavenly meaning will follow.

Does all this Bible interpretation sound like a lot of work? Just remember the rewards that await you. Think of the spiritual growth that is just around the corner. Consider how God will be able to use this knowledge and insight to make you a more useful tool in His hands. In the spirit of creative communication, allow me to finish this chapter with a parable:

A man was out walking in the desert when a voice said to him, "Pick up some pebbles and put them in your pocket. Tomorrow you will be both sorry and glad." The man obeyed. He stooped down and picked up a handful of pebbles and put them in his pocket. The next morning he reached into his pocket and found diamonds and rubies and emeralds. He was both glad and sorry. Glad that he had taken some—sorry that he hadn't taken more. Don't miss out on the riches of God. Reach into the Bible and fill your heart with the jewels of His Word.

7

APPLICATION: OPENING YOUR HEART

Some Bible teaching is like swimming lessons on dry land. We have been taught all the things commanded by the Great Commission, but we do not observe them. Some know so much doctrine that an encyclopedia could not hold it, but what they know by experience could be put in a pocket notebook. We are afflicted with rocking chair religion and shade tree theology. We are like a man whose suitcase is covered with foreign hotel labels but who has never been out of his home state. —VANCE HAVNER

AN AGNOSTIC college professor was visiting a village in the Fiji Islands where the gospel had penetrated. He remarked to an elderly chief, "You're a great leader, but it's a pity you've been taken in by foreign missionaries who only want to get rich through you. No one believes the Bible anymore. People are tired of the threadbare story of Christ dying on a cross for the sins of mankind."

The old chief, himself a believer, answered the professor by saying, "See that great rock over there? We used to smash the heads of our victims on it. In that oven next to it, we roasted the bodies of our enemies. If it hadn't been for those good missionaries, the Bible, and the love of Jesus, we would still be cannibals, and you would probably be our supper."

I'm sure at that point the professor was thrilled that this tribe had not only read the Bible but also applied it to their daily lives.

In the preceding chapters we have seen the importance of observation and interpretation in our study of the Bible. However, if we stop there, all our work will have been in vain. It's the *application* of Scripture that makes the difference in our lives. Application is where the rubber meets the road. Whenever I hear Christians say, "I want to go somewhere where I can get into the meat of the Word; I don't want this milk stuff," I'm inclined to remind them of what Jesus said: "My meat is to do the will of him that sent Me" (John 4:34, KJV). The meat of the Word is doing what God wants. That's why observation and interpretation must always lead to application.

Jesus told a story of two builders, both of whom constructed nice homes. Although both houses looked great from the outside, one of them lacked an essential element—a foundation! Of all the places to scrimp, the foundation is certainly not the one to choose. Then Jesus applied his story in a powerful way:

> Therefore whoever hears these sayings of Mine, and does them, I will liken him to a wise man who built his house on the rock: and the rain descended, the floods came, and the

> winds blew and beat on that house; and it did not fall, for it was founded on the rock. But everyone who hears these sayings of Mine, and does not do them, will be like a foolish man who built his house on the sand: and the rain descended, the floods came, and the winds blew and beat on that house; and it fell. And great was its fall. (MATTHEW 7:24-27)

In this passage, Jesus gives an example that can be used to illustrate the difference between merely studying the Bible and applying what we've learned to our lives. It's easy to be intoxicated by biblical knowledge, and we can even become reckless and prideful with it. We must allow our knowledge *about* God to be transformed into a knowledge *of* God. J. I. Packer reminds us, "If we pursue theological knowledge for its own sake, it is bound to go bad on us. It will make us proud and conceited." We must guard our hearts against such foolishness. We've all observed how wine can cause an introvert to become overly confident and say things he would normally be ashamed to say. Biblical knowledge can have a similar effect, puffing us up, leading us to try to impress others with our mastery of Scripture. But unless we love other people and live according to what the Lord has taught us, the Bible says we are "nothing," even though we might "understand all mysteries and all knowledge" (1 Corinthians 13:2).

Some people become experts in the Scriptures, yet their lives are unchanged. I once visited a friend who had recently completed seminary. He could quote the theologians and give chapter and verse from the Bible for every situation, but after a couple of hours he looked at me sadly and said, "Skip, I don't think I know the Lord anymore." He explained that his seminary training had placed a huge emphasis on intellectual knowledge, but almost none on prayer, intercession, or pleasing and loving Jesus Christ. It was knowledge for knowledge' sake, and it led him to spiritual emptiness. His study of the Bible became just another discipline, like studying mathematics or science. In the end, what good does it do to have a full head and an empty heart?

The goal of studying the Bible is not simply observation, or even interpretation; rather it is application. The point is not to uncover a new tidbit of knowledge about prophecy or explain the precise definition of a Greek word. The joy comes in applying the truth to our own lives. Only then can we see that the Bible works! History tells us that when Crowfoot, chief of the Blackfoot nation in southern Alberta, gave the Canadian Pacific Railway permission to lay track from Medicine Hat to Calgary, he was given a lifetime railroad pass in exchange for those rights. Chief Crowfoot reportedly put the pass in a leather pouch and wore it around his neck for the rest of his life—but he never once availed himself of the rights and privileges it spelled out. What a tragic loss when Christians use the Bible as mere decoration, rather than turn it loose to work in their lives.

THREE NECESSARY CONDITIONS OF THE HEART

Application begins with our willingness to respond to what we read. We must be ready to submit ourselves to the all-encompassing principles found in Scripture. From there, we can focus on the transforming process of applying God's specific truths to our lives. But first, our hearts must conform to three necessary conditions:

1. We Must Be His

The first, and most obvious, condition is that we must belong to Christ. If we find the Bible too difficult to understand or if, when we read it, it doesn't make any sense, the problem may be that our hearts have not been changed. We must be spiritually awakened before we can develop a spiritual appetite. Life always precedes growth. The apostle Paul put it this way: "But the natural man does not receive the things of the Spirit of God, for they are foolishness to him; nor can he know them, because they are spiritually discerned" (1 Corinthians 2:14). First, we must make sure we have a personal relationship with God through Jesus Christ. If you're not sure, then stop right now, admit that you are a sinner, and ask God to forgive you based on the finished work of Jesus Christ on the cross. Receive Jesus as your Savior and Lord, and then you'll be ready to start fresh.

2. We Must Be Hungry

Jesus said, "Blessed are those who hunger and thirst for righteousness, for they shall be filled" (Matthew 5:6). Notice that Jesus promises to feed those who are truly hungry, not those looking for a casual snack. The apostle Peter later added this advice: "As newborn babes, desire the pure milk of the word, that you may grow thereby, if indeed you have tasted that the Lord is gracious"

(1 Peter 2:2-3). A spiritual appetite is a prerequisite for spiritual feeding. If we're not hungry, we won't eat. If we're not aware of our need for God, we won't pursue Him. The Bible says that God rewards those who diligently seek Him (Hebrews 11:6). If our hearts are hungry, we will regard the Scriptures as precious food. Ask God for a voracious appetite for His Word.

3. *We Must Be Humble*

Once we have developed an appetite for the Word, there must be a humble willingness to obey it. The best way to approach the Bible is as an obedient servant waiting for the master to give instructions. Our willingness to put the Lord's instructions into practice shows that we are in submission to Him as our Lord and Master. Studying the Bible is exciting when we are prepared to apply its truth in obedience. As God told Joshua, "This Book of the Law shall not depart from your mouth, but you shall meditate in it day and night, that you may observe to do according to all that is written in it. For then you will make your way prosperous, and then you will have good success" (Joshua 1:8).

RESPONDING BOLDLY TO GOD'S WORD

I read in *USA Today* about some Harvard astronomers who have "dialed" outer space and are waiting for an answer. Their receiver, located near Boston, is a sophisticated, computerized dish, measuring eighty-five feet in diameter, that allows the scientists to listen to and analyze 128,000 frequencies at once, 24 hours a day. According to the article, this endeavor, which is expected to last for four years, is the most extensive search ever conducted for intelligent life in outer space. I wonder how many Christians listen for God's voice with as much determination and expectation?

God speaks, but we must listen, and we must listen attentively. Then we must respond boldly. This bold obedience should begin early in our Christian life so that responding to God's truth becomes a habit. The following acrostic, **B-O-L-D,** can help us remember the process of applying Scripture to our lives:

Believe God's declarations of truth.
Obey His commandments.
Learn from examples in Scripture.
Declare God's promises as our own.

BELIEVE GOD'S DECLARATIONS OF TRUTH

The Bible is full of declarations that are unencumbered by any promise, condition, warning, or challenge. When we encounter these blanket statements, the proper response is simply to believe what God has said. For example, the Bible declares that God is love—no debate, no qualifying circumstances. Accepting these truths at face value will help to frame our understanding of the nature and character of God.

In Psalm 19, we find a blanket statement of God's sovereignty over creation: "The heavens declare the glory of God; and the firmament shows His handiwork. Day unto day utters speech, and night unto night reveals knowledge. There is no speech nor language where their voice is not heard. Their line has gone out through all the earth, and their words to the end of the world" (Psalm 19:1-4). These straightforward declarations reveal the very nature of God and remind us that His glory and creative genius are clearly reflected in creation. Because we're all surrounded by God's creation, this message reaches everyone on earth—and faith is the only proper response. And as we respond to the Lord in faith, our faith itself is strengthened.

Sometimes what we read in the Bible will fly in the face of modern philosophy. That's okay. We must measure our society by the yardstick of Scripture, not the other way around. We don't have to dance around the differences or defend God's wisdom. Dwight Hall outlined the following comparisons to illustrate the primacy of Scripture:

SOME SAY: "Everyone is basically good."
GOD SAYS: "All have sinned" (ROMANS 3:23, NIV).

SOME SAY: "There is no hell, so there's no need to be concerned."
GOD SAYS: "Fear him who . . . has power to throw you into hell" (LUKE 12:5, NIV).

SOME SAY: "Heaven is not a real place."
GOD SAYS: "I go to prepare a place for you" (JOHN 14:2, NASB).

SOME SAY: "There is no such thing as life after death."
GOD SAYS: "Man is destined to die . . . and after that . . . judgment" (HEBREWS 9:27, NIV).

SOME SAY: "We can do nothing about the future. What is going to be will be."

GOD SAYS: "You must be born again" (JOHN 3:7). How can you be born again? "Whoever confesses and renounces [his sins] finds mercy" (PROVERBS 28:13, NIV). "To all who received [Christ]. . . he gave the right to become children of God" (JOHN 1:12, NIV).

SOME SAY: "We cannot be sure of salvation or our destiny when we die."

GOD SAYS: "You may know that you have eternal life" (1 JOHN 5:13).

OBEY HIS COMMANDMENTS

Many times in the Bible, God commands us to do something or avoid doing something. If we fail to obey, we suffer the consequences. For example, Jesus said that we must be born again. He didn't say that we should consider rebirth as an option, He said it was an imperative: We *must* be born again. And if we aren't? "Jesus answered and said to him, 'Most assuredly, I say to you, unless one is born again, he cannot see the kingdom of God'" (John 3:3).

Another example is the commandment for us to repent of our sins: "The time is fulfilled, and the kingdom of God is at hand. Repent, and believe in the gospel" (Mark 1:15). I once heard someone say, "Oh Lord, forgive my hang-ups." Listen, God is not in the business of forgiving "hang-ups." He forgives sins. We must be willing to recognize our sin for what it is and obediently bring it before

God in repentance. Repentance is not an option; it's a commandment. Even after we come to Christ, there will be areas in our lives that require repentance. God will reveal areas in our lives that need to change. Repentance means being willing to turn away from those actions, attitudes, or patterns of behavior that offend God.

Does every commandment apply to us? There are times in the Bible when God singles out an individual or a group and commands them to do something specific. If there is no direct application to us, how do we regard these commands? Let's look at an example from Matthew 19:16-21:

> Now behold, one came and said to Him, "Good Teacher, what good thing shall I do that I may have eternal life?" So He said to him, "Why do you call Me good? No one is good but One, that is, God. But if you want to enter into life, keep the commandments." He said to Him, "Which ones?" Jesus said, "'You shall not murder,' 'You shall not commit adultery,' 'You shall not steal,' 'You shall not bear false witness,' 'Honor your father and your mother,' and, 'You shall love your neighbor as yourself.'" The young man said to Him, "All these things I have kept from my youth. What do I still lack?" Jesus said to him, "If you want to be perfect, go, sell what you have and give to the poor, and you will have treasure in heaven; and come, follow Me."

In telling this young man to sell everything he had, Jesus gave specific instructions to a particular person in a certain condition.

Because Jesus knew that the man's possessions were a hindrance to him, He told him to sell what he had. Judging from the context, and by the way the young man responded, we can see that his wealth had become his god: "But when the young man heard that saying, he went away sorrowful, for he had great possessions" (Matthew 19:22).

Money and possessions may not be a hindrance for us. We might even be broke, or perhaps we use our money to give to those in need. Does that mean we can skip over this story in our study of the Bible? No, because even though the specific details might not apply to us, we can still uncover the underlying principle and apply it to our lives. Although this command was given to a specific individual, it is based on a timeless principle that we find repeated throughout Christ's teaching: We must rid our lives of anything that hinders our relationship with God—anything that has become an idol or a master passion. It may not be money. It may be a relationship with someone or a position of power on the corporate ladder. By going to the root of the commandment, we can identify the principle and draw our own personal application.

LEARN FROM EXAMPLES IN SCRIPTURE

Looking at living examples from the Bible allows us to see flesh and blood illustrations of both positive and negative behavior. When the Bible tells us about its heroes, it doesn't hide their flaws—the fact that they often floundered, fumbled, and made huge mistakes. Think of King David's life, for example. Before he repented, he was an adulterer, a murderer, even a terrorist, yet

God called him a man after His own heart. I take great hope in that! We see a tenderness in David that is rare even among God's people. In Psalm 27 we find a beautiful example of David's open heart and his responsiveness before the Lord:

> The Lord is my light and my salvation; whom shall I fear? The Lord is the strength of my life; of whom shall I be afraid? . . . One thing I have desired of the Lord, that will I seek: That I may dwell in the house of the Lord all the days of my life, to behold the beauty of the Lord, and to inquire in His temple. . . . When You said, "Seek My face," my heart said to You, "Your face, Lord, I will seek." . . . When my father and my mother forsake me, then the Lord will take care of me. (PSALM 27:1, 4, 8, 10)

What an awesome example of love and trust in the Lord! Though David was a flawed vessel in many ways, he continually returned to prayer and worshiping God. His words are an example of the way we should present our hearts before the Lord. Also, his prayer of repentance after his sin with Bathsheba (see Psalm 51) is a sterling example of contrite remorse before God. So it is that we learn from the example of God's people throughout the Scriptures, those saints who comprise "so great a cloud of witnesses" in Hebrews 12:1. As we read the stories of others who have run the race before us, their example should inspire us to think, *If they can do it, then by God's grace, so can I.*

Scripture also contains numerous examples of what we should

avoid. King Saul demonstrates the ugliness of pride and rebellion (see 1 Samuel 15:17, 22-24). Solomon's life is an example of dissatisfaction and the consequences of idolatry (see Ecclesiastes 2:1-10 and 1 Kings 11:4). Judas Iscariot is the epitome of religious hypocrisy: a man who seemed so close to Jesus but was lost (see John 13:10-11; 17:12). In 1 Corinthians 10:6-11, the apostle Paul refers to the children of Israel as examples of what *not* to do (they happened to fit that calling quite well):

> Now these things became our examples, to the intent that we should not lust after evil things as they also lusted. And do not become idolaters as were some of them. As it is written, "The people sat down to eat and drink, and rose up to play." Nor let us commit sexual immorality, as some of them did, and in one day twenty-three thousand fell; nor let us tempt Christ, as some of them also tempted, and were destroyed by serpents; nor complain, as some of them also complained, and were destroyed by the destroyer. Now all these things happened to them as examples, and they were written for our admonition, upon whom the ends of the ages have come.

The message is clear: Learn from these bad examples—and don't do what they did. Remember George Santayana's famous maxim: "Those who do not remember the past are condemned to repeat it." We remember the past well when we look for good examples to follow and avoid the mistakes of others.

DECLARE GOD'S PROMISES AS OUR OWN

In 1956, *Time* magazine carried an article about a schoolteacher named Everett R. Storms of Kitchner, Canada, who, after his twenty-seventh reading of the Bible, decided to tally up all the promises in the Bible. This formidable task took about eighteen months, and Storms came up with 7,487 promises that God has made to man. In our application of Scripture, how are we to regard these promises?

A popular creed these days is to "find a promise and claim it!" However, there's more to claiming a promise than announcing, "I take that promise, amen." To claim a Scripture requires an open heart and a willingness to accept whatever God's will might bring in conjunction with the promise. Some of God's promises are assurances of blessing, whereas other promises are assurances of judgment and punishment. We must remember that even these negative promises carry just as much weight as the popular positive ones that everybody loves to quote.

There are two kinds of promises in the Bible: unconditional and conditional. An unconditional promise is when God says He will do something regardless of our actions. It is the declaration of a certain purpose of God, which will be fulfilled in God's way and time. The covenant God made with Noah, for example, was an unconditional covenant with unconditional promises. It revealed God's purpose for the human race subsequent to Noah:

> And God said: "This is the sign of the covenant which I make between Me and you, and every living creature that is with

> you, for perpetual generations: I set My rainbow in the cloud, and it shall be for the sign of the covenant between Me and the earth. It shall be, when I bring a cloud over the earth, that the rainbow shall be seen in the cloud; and I will remember My covenant which is between Me and you and every living creature of all flesh; the waters shall never again become a flood to destroy all flesh." (GENESIS 9:12-15)

God also made unconditional promises to Abraham. He said He would bring personal blessing to Abraham and make a great nation emerge through his descendants. Through Abraham, blessings would come to the whole world: "I will make you a great nation; I will bless you and make your name great; and you shall be a blessing. I will bless those who bless you, and I will curse him who curses you; and in you all the families of the earth shall be blessed" (Genesis 12:2-3). Abraham didn't have to do anything to warrant these promises; God gave them with no strings attached.

Conditional promises, on the other hand, consist of two parts: God's and ours. God promises to do something for us if we do what He requires. We cannot separate the promise from the condition without distorting the message and its intent. Many promises in the Bible are conditional, contingent on the little word *if*. One Old Testament example is found in Deuteronomy 28, where God promises the nation of Israel blessings and fruitfulness "*if* you diligently obey the voice of the Lord your God, to observe carefully all His commandments" (verse 1, emphasis mine). But He also showed them the other side of the coin: *If* they were unfaithful and disobedient, it would negate the promises and result in curses (verse 15).

Let's look at a familiar New Testament promise found in Philippians 4:19: "And my God shall supply all of your need according to His riches in glory by Christ Jesus." The four verses immediately preceding verse 19 reveal the conditions attached to this promise. As Paul traveled on his missionary journey, the Philippians had faithfully and sacrificially contributed to his support. Because of their selfless care for him as He served God, Paul said they would experience God's care and provision for their own needs. Lifting the promise out of its context alters the message.

When we come across a promise in Scripture that has an attached condition, we have no right to lay claim to it unless we are obedient to the terms. We can't just underline the part we like and say, "I claim it. I stand on it, in Jesus' name. It's mine, that settles it." We have to be willing to meet our responsibility—to obey the commandments and then claim the promises.

William Penn, founder of the commonwealth of Pennsylvania, was popular with the local Native Americans. One time they told him that he could have as much of their land as he could encompass on foot in a single day. So, early the next morning, he started out and walked until late that night. When he went to claim his land, the Indians were greatly surprised because they really didn't think he would take them seriously. But they kept their promise and gave him a large parcel of land, which today is part of the city of Philadelphia. William Penn simply believed what they said and acted accordingly. How many of God's promises are left untapped because we don't believe them and act on them?

TRANSFORMING YOUR QUIET TIMES OF STUDY

It's early morning and the house is quiet. You sit down with your Bible and your notebook, anxious to spend time with God in His Word. You are prepared. You have prayed for an attitude of receptivity and sacrificial devotion. You know the steps of observation and the process of interpretation. Now you want to lift God's truths off the page and into your heart by applying them to your life. But how? Sometimes we understand something on an intellectual or conceptual level, but we get confused when it's time to act on our knowledge. The following guidelines for self-examination will take the edge off the mystery of applying God's Word. In the context of the Scripture you are studying, ask yourself:

1. How does this passage apply to my life? How does it apply to my family, my job, my nation, and my other relationships?
2. What changes must I make? In light of the truth in these verses, is there something I must start doing or stop doing?
3. How will I carry out these changes? What is my plan of action?
4. What will be my personal prayer concerning this truth?
5. Which verse or verses in this section should I memorize?
6. What illustration or word picture will help me remember what I've read?

In this vital phase of our study—application—we leave the role of student and step into the role of heart surgeon. We have only one patient, and it's one whom we know very well, because the ailing heart is our own. We will examine our hearts under the revealing light of Scripture, searching for areas of sin and weakness and devising plans to correct and strengthen those areas. God is the Master Surgeon directing the operation through His Holy Spirit, and we will lift up our concerns and repentance in prayer to the Great Physician for His healing, guiding touch. Finally, we will hide God's Word in our hearts to keep us from future sin.

8

PRACTICING WHAT WE'VE PREACHED

KNOWING HOW TO STUDY the Bible is one thing; doing it regularly is something else. In teaching His disciples about servanthood, Jesus remarked, "If you know these things, blessed [or happy] are you if you *do* them" (John 13:17, emphasis mine). The same principle can be applied to our study of the Bible. Our enjoyment—our blessing—comes in the process of *doing* it.

To solidify our understanding of how to enjoy studying the Bible through the processes we've discussed, let's practice on a familiar passage of Scripture: the story in John 4 of Jesus and the woman at the well of Samaria. You may already be acquainted with this story, but let's take a fresh look at it together and discover what truths might lie beneath the surface.

[3][Jesus] left Judea and departed again to Galilee.

[4]But He needed to go through Samaria. [5]So He came to a city of Samaria which is called Sychar, near the plot of ground that Jacob gave to his son Joseph. [6]Now Jacob's well was there. Jesus therefore, being wearied from His journey, sat thus by the well. It was about the sixth hour. [7]A woman of Samaria came to draw water. Jesus said to her, "Give Me a drink." [8]For His disciples had gone away into the city to buy food.

[9]Then the woman of Samaria said to Him, "How is it that You, being a Jew, ask a drink from me, a Samaritan woman?" For Jews have no dealings with Samaritans.

[10]Jesus answered and said to her, "If you knew the gift of God, and who it is who says to you, 'Give Me a drink,' you would have asked Him, and He would have given you living water."

[11]The woman said to Him, "Sir, You have nothing to draw with, and the well is deep. Where then do You get that living water? [12]Are You greater than our father Jacob, who gave us the well, and drank from it himself, as well as his sons and his livestock?"

[13]Jesus answered and said to her, "Whoever drinks of this water will thirst again, [14]but whoever drinks of the water that I shall give him will never thirst. But the water that I shall give him will become in him a fountain of water springing up into everlasting life."

[15]The woman said to Him, "Sir, give me this water, that I may not thirst, nor come here to draw."

[16]Jesus said to her, "Go, call your husband, and come here."

[17]The woman answered and said, "I have no husband."

Jesus said to her, "You have well said, 'I have no husband,' [18]for you have had five husbands, and the one whom you now have is not your husband; in that you spoke truly."

[19]The woman said to Him, "Sir, I perceive that You are a prophet. [20]Our fathers worshiped on this mountain, and you Jews say that in Jerusalem is the place where one ought to worship."

[21]Jesus said to her, "Woman, believe Me, the hour is coming when you will neither on this mountain, nor in Jerusalem, worship the Father. [22]You worship what you do not know; we know what we worship, for salvation is of the Jews. [23]But the hour is coming, and now is, when the true worshipers will worship the Father in spirit and truth; for the Father is seeking such to worship Him. [24]God is Spirit, and those who worship Him must worship in spirit and truth."

[25]The woman said to Him, "I know that Messiah is coming" (who is called Christ). "When He comes, He will tell us all things."

[26]Jesus said to her, "I who speak to you am He."

[27]And at this point His disciples came, and they marveled that He talked with a woman; yet no one said, "What do You seek?" or, "Why are You talking with her?" [28]The woman then left her waterpot, went her way into the city, and said to the men, [29]"Come, see a Man who told me all

things that I ever did. Could this be the Christ?" [30]Then they went out of the city and came to Him.

[31]In the meantime His disciples urged Him, saying, "Rabbi, eat."

[32]But He said to them, "I have food to eat of which you do not know."

[33]Therefore the disciples said to one another, "Has anyone brought Him anything to eat?"

[34]Jesus said to them, "My food is to do the will of Him who sent Me, and to finish His work. [35]Do you not say, 'There are still four months and then comes the harvest'? Behold, I say to you, lift up your eyes and look at the fields, for they are already white for harvest! [36]And he who reaps receives wages, and gathers fruit for eternal life, that both he who sows and he who reaps may rejoice together. [37]For in this the saying is true: 'One sows and another reaps.' [38]I sent you to reap that for which you have not labored; others have labored, and you have entered into their labors."

[39]And many of the Samaritans of that city believed in Him because of the word of the woman who testified, "He told me all that I ever did." [40]So when the Samaritans had come to Him, they urged Him to stay with them; and He stayed there two days. [41]And many more believed because of His own word. [42]Then they said to the woman, "Now we believe, not because of what you said, for we ourselves have heard Him and we know that this is indeed the Christ, the Savior of the world."

PRACTICING OUR OBSERVATION SKILLS

Now that we've read through the passage, let's begin the process of observation by answering the six basic journalistic questions we discussed in chapter 4:

1. *Who* is involved in this passage? Jesus, a Samaritan woman, Jesus' disciples, and the Samaritan population from the nearby town.

2. *When* did these events take place? When Jesus was traveling from Jerusalem (in Judea, the southern portion of the land of Israel) to Galilee (in the northern part of Israel, where He lived most of the time). The time of day is also mentioned, in verse 6. The sixth hour (which is noontime) is getting toward the hottest time of the day, when typically one would be seeking refreshment in the shade, rather than lugging a heavy water jug out to the town well. Women usually drew water early in the day before the sun got too hot.

3. *Where* did these events take place? In the region of Samaria, near the city of Sychar, at a well that had been dug by Jacob (verses 3-6, 12).

4. *What* is going on in the story? Jesus is taking a break from His journey and sits down by the well of Jacob. The disciples have gone on ahead into Sychar to shop for food. A Samaritan woman comes out to draw water at the well, and Jesus has the opportunity to speak directly to the need in her life, without interruption or interference from any onlookers.

5. *How* does Jesus approach the woman? With a simple appeal to human kindness. The direct address was customary: "Give me a

drink" (verse 7), but the woman is surprised that a Jewish rabbi would even speak to her, a Samaritan woman. Jesus uses this opportunity to draw her into a conversation by comparing ordinary water (which she understood) with spiritual refreshment (which she desperately needed). It was enough to pique her curiosity and prompt further inquiry. With each turn of the conversation, Jesus draws her in until she comes face-to-face with her need for the Messiah.

6. *Why* was Jesus here? The text tells us (in verse 4) that Jesus *needed* to be here, which indicates that this was not a coincidental stopover but rather a planned event.

DIGGING DEEPER

Now that we've made these simple observations, let's dig a bit deeper and observe the text more carefully.

Are There Any Repeated Words or Phrases?

Seven times our attention is drawn to the phrases "through Samaria," "of Samaria," "Samaritan woman," or "Samaritans." The author obviously wants us to know that Jesus isn't just meeting with a group of Israelites, but a special group from a specific area. Also, variations of the word *drink* occur six times, and *water* or *living* water is used seven times. There is a definite emphasis on quenching thirst here—and the analogy of physical thirst to spiritual thirst is clearly indicated. Jesus used the natural need for physical refreshment to illustrate his offer to satisfy and refresh the Samaritans at a deeper level.

Are There Any Peculiar Words or Phrases?

The word *Messiah* is unfamiliar to many in the Western world. Although it has found its way into our vocabulary, the meaning of *Messiah* has dramatically changed from its original intent. Apparently the Samaritans anticipated the coming of a person who would reveal everything they needed to understand about the right way to worship God (verse 25). "Messiah" is the same basic title as "Christ" (verses 25 and 42). If you have a Bible dictionary, it would be helpful to look these terms up and compare them.

Are There Any Comparisons and Contrasts?

The first two verses of our text present an important opening contrast. "[Jesus] left Judea and departed again to Galilee. But He needed to go through Samaria." This information is noteworthy because the normal route from Judea to Galilee didn't run through Samaria. Something other than ease of travel was driving Jesus to that location—and His purpose quickly became clear: to influence and encourage this neglected and ill-regarded group of people.

One of the main comparisons in the text is that between water, which only quenches thirst temporarily, and "living water," which Jesus indicates will satisfy eternal longings.

The woman at the well draws attention to the contrast between Jewish and Samaritan places and styles of worship. Jesus transcends the comparison and redirects the woman's focus to a greater issue—the worship of the Father in spirit and in truth.

Are There Any Figurative Expressions?

One obvious metaphor that Jesus uses is the term "living water." Expanding on the well-understood relationship between thirst and refreshment, Jesus establishes the truth that this "gift of God" (verse 10) can become an internal source of refreshment that will endure continuously in its capacity to satisfy (verse 14).

Another figure of speech that Jesus employs is the phrase "the hour is coming," which points to an indeterminate time in the future, not necessarily a fixed sixty-minute block of time.

Is There Anything Strange in This Passage?

One strange feature of this story is that Jesus, upon meeting the Samaritan woman for the first time, is able to reveal a comprehensive knowledge of her past marital relationships (verses 16-19). Christians who are familiar and comfortable with the deity of Christ may not find this supernatural insight strange, but it certainly would be to a first-time reader—and it was even more remarkable to the woman at the well! If we allow this strange conversation to have its full impact on us, it will make our study of Christ's teaching even more forceful and life changing.

Picturing Ourselves in the Scene

The day is warmer than usual. I am sitting on a rock just under a eucalyptus tree that stands about thirty yards from the well that Jacob dug hundreds of years ago. It's noontime and a solitary woman is making her way along the dusty path leading out from the nearby village. Perched on her shoulder is a large jug for fetching water. As she approaches the well, she notices a man leaning up against the stones. He has obviously been walking a long time. Sweat covers his face and a weary look creases his brow. Having no bowl to lower down into the well, he asks the woman to give him a drink. Her answer is surprisingly abrupt.

"You're a Jew, I'm a Samaritan, one of those people you don't associate with. Why would you even ask me for a helping hand?"

The man's reply is calm but piercing. His words seem strange, as if he's in another world! "If you knew who I was, you'd be the one asking me for water that would quench your thirst forever!"

What does he mean? I wonder as I brush away a buzzing swarm of flies. *He's just thirsty and tired—and judging by his words, perhaps a bit delirious.*

The woman's response is again curt. "You don't have anything to hold water in. So how are you going to get the 'living water' you speak of?" Her terse words are accompanied by a sneer developed over many years of dealing with men.

"You'll get thirsty again, you know," the stranger replies. "You'll be right back here again tomorrow. But I have a source of refreshment that you will find so satisfying you'll never want anything else."

I lean forward on the rock where I'm perched. This is the most interesting conversation I've ever heard—especially around these parts. *Who is this guy, anyway?*

The callous Samaritan woman isn't quite as impressed. She answers the man with a smart-alecky response, "What, are you greater than Jacob, who dug this well? I'm just dying to hear where to get this unusual water you say you have. Just think, I won't have to walk out here every day in this heat!"

At this the stranger abruptly changes his tone. "Get your husband!"

The woman stops and looks directly into his eyes. "I'm not married," she bites back.

Why did he tell her that? I muse. But before I can ponder the thought any further, the man says something that disarms the woman and takes my breath away.

"You're right about that. Although you've been married five times in the past, right now you're living with a man who's not your husband."

Now I recognize the woman. She's the one that everyone in town knows as being a bit "loose." She's been married so many times that she has probably forgotten the names of all her husbands by now. *But how on earth would this stranger know anything about the woman's past?*

That's exactly what the woman would like to know. "Who are you?" she says. "You must be a prophet or something." Seizing the opportunity of being with such an unusual and spiritually insightful person, she launches into a discussion of religion and the coming Messiah. Although her life has been far from spiritual, she is thirsty to know more. She says she expects that one day a Messiah will come and then we'll know if the Jews were right or the Samaritans were right.

"That day is today," the stranger calmly declares. "You're looking at the Messiah."

My throat is dry from not swallowing for the last few minutes. A surge of adrenaline shoots through my system as I try to take in all this information. *Am I hearing correctly? What did he just say? Could it be possible?* As these thoughts whir inside my head, the woman drops the water pot and runs back toward the village. But she's not running in fear; she is running with excitement.

You may choose not to embellish the details in exactly the same way, but you can see how picturing yourself in the scene really brings the story to life. The more time you spend combing through the text and noticing what it really says, the more you'll be amazed at how much you can glean. And the more you observe, the more you'll have to work with when it comes to interpreting and applying the Scriptures.

PRACTICING OUR INTERPRETATION

Now that we have compiled a significant number of observations, let's go back through the text using the five interpretative questions we discussed in chapter 5.

What Is the Context?

The *immediate context* of this passage from John 4 is Jesus' decision to go out of His way to bring the good news of salvation to the Samaritan city of Sychar. He then works within the context of a common daily activity (drawing water from a well) to introduce the life-changing principle of "living water." When the disciples return from their grocery shopping trip into Sychar,

Jesus adapts the immediate context of food and expands it in order to initiate a discussion of evangelism, which he bases on another common activity, namely the planting and harvesting of grain.

The *remote context* sheds additional light on our understanding of Jesus' purpose in going to Jacob's well. If we consider the first four chapters of the Gospel of John, we see that John has been writing about Jesus' public ministry and the spread of His message throughout the land of Israel. Through a series of vignettes similar in scope to the story of the woman at the well, John emphasizes the theme of salvation and shows us the reactions of various groups of people: John the Baptist (see John 1:29-34; 3:22-36); Andrew, Philip, Peter, and Nathanael, all of whom became disciples (see John 1:35-51); the townspeople of Cana in Galilee (see John 2:1-12); the people of Judea—and especially Jerusalem (see John 2:13–3:21); and finally, as we have seen in John 4, the Samaritans.

What Do the Words Mean?

Certain words in the text require a closer look. Let's consider a few of the main ones. Perhaps the most prominent is the term "living water." Using cross-references and our concordance, we discover an Old Testament reference in the book of Jeremiah. "For My people have committed two evils: They have forsaken Me, the fountain of living waters, and hewn themselves cisterns—broken cisterns that can hold no water" (Jeremiah 2:13). Also, the prophets Zechariah and Ezekiel anticipated a time when "living waters shall flow from Jerusalem" (Zechariah 14:8; Ezekiel 47:9). We can see that Jesus used an existing metaphor to speak of the inner refreshment and cleansing that comes from having eternal life and knowing God in a covenant relationship.

In John 4:24, when Jesus speaks of worshipping God "in spirit and truth," we might wonder whether He is referring to the human spirit or the Holy Spirit. A quick concordance search of how the phrase "in spirit" is used elsewhere in Scripture shows that Jesus intends for us to understand the role of the human spirit in our worship. His main point is that our worship is not to be merely outward (by external conformity to religious rituals and attendance at specific places, such as the mountain of Samaria or the temple in Jerusalem) but inward—"in spirit"—having the proper attitude of heart.

The word *Messiah* is another term we might want to research. Most Bible dictionaries will tell us that the word means "anointed one" and refers to the long-anticipated arrival of one who would deliver God's people and establish His kingdom. The term was originally thought to refer to a conquering Messiah, which is why many followers of Jesus expected Him to overthrow the Roman government and set up the kingdom immediately. Although the Old Testament does predict a conquering Messiah, we now understand that these prophecies will be fulfilled at Christ's second coming. The Samaritans believed that Messiah would return to rebuild their temple in Samaria and reinstitute their sacrificial system for universal recognition.

What Does the Grammar Show?

When the disciples returned with the food they had purchased in Sychar, they were amazed to find Jesus talking to a woman (verse 27). Why should that amaze them? First, because it was a breach of social custom among religious Jews for a Jewish man to speak to a woman in public; but also because He didn't stop to include the disciples in the conversation. How do we know this? Here is where an understanding of grammar plays a part. The word for "speaking" is a verb set in the imperfect tense, which denotes a continuation of activity. So in other words, when the disciples returned with the food, Jesus "kept on speaking" to the woman. Her spiritual need was far more important than His own physical need to eat!

What Is the Background?

A good Bible dictionary or a book on ancient Hebrew culture and customs will reveal some useful information not disclosed by John in the text of his Gospel. For one thing, the Jews and Samaritans hated one another. In the eyes of the Jews, the Samaritans were "half-breeds" because they were the descendants of ancient Jews who had populated the region and intermarried with the pagan Assyrians. After many bitter years of contention, the Samaritans established a separate place of worship by building a temple (apart from the temple in Jerusalem) on Mount Gerizim. The woman at the well had been raised to believe that the Gerizim temple was the only true house of worship.

Most Jews wouldn't travel through Samaria. No roads were established or maintained to promote commerce with Israel. This information sheds light on the woman's statement to Jesus that "the Jews have no dealings with the Samaritans," and it underscores our understanding that Jesus made a deliberate, out-of-the-way trip to Sychar. He didn't care about people's expectations or customary dealings—especially when they were based on sinful prejudice. He "needed" to go to Samaria because He knew that His meeting with the woman at the well would change not only her own life but the lives of many others in the region.

Does Our Interpretation Balance with the Rest of Scripture?

We've already seen how the phrase "living water" carries over from the Old Testament to the New Testament. By looking up key phrases in other parts of the Bible we gain a consistent, well-rounded understanding of what they mean. Further, when we see how a word or phrase is used throughout Scripture, it keeps us from jumping to conclusions and assigning an erroneous interpretation to the verses we are studying.

The picture of Jesus going to the "forbidden area" of Samaria is consistent with His purpose in coming to earth as a man. John tells us that "God so loved the world [not just the Jews to the exclusion of the Samaritans, or Gentiles—like most of us!] that He gave His only begotten Son, that whoever believes in Him should not perish but have everlasting life" (John 3:16). The apostle Paul made this argument even more explicit. "After all, God is not the God of the Jews only, is he? Isn't he also the God of the Gentiles? Of course he is. There is only one God, and there is only one way of being accepted by him. He makes people right with himself only by faith, whether they are Jews or Gentiles" (Romans 3:29-30, NLT).

What about the idea that our worship is not to be focused on a location or a ritual but must be something inward, "in spirit," from the heart? This concept, too, is consistent with the rest of Scripture. The prophet Isaiah and Jesus both mentioned our tendency to promote outward ritual to the exclusion of an inward relationship with God. "Therefore the Lord said: . . . 'These people draw near with their mouths and honor Me with their lips, but have removed their hearts far from Me'" (Isaiah 29:13).

PRACTICING OUR APPLICATION

Now that we've applied our skills of *observation* and *interpretation* to the story of Jesus and the woman at the well, we're ready to practice our skills of *application*. To illustrate this step, I'll share some of my own reflections on this story.

1. How Does This Passage Apply to My Life?

The first thing that strikes me as I read this story is that it doesn't matter *where* I worship as much as it matters *that* I worship the true and living God. I could be in an ornate sanctuary with stained glass windows, a storefront church building, my home, my garage, or my car. I could worship with a guitar, piano, organ, or with no music at all. The externals of worship don't matter. It's not the *art* of worship that is vital; it's the *heart* of worship that counts. Certainly, I must worship according to God's directives, but the important issue is that my heart is involved and that I'm not focused on outward appearances. There must be sincerity and truth. The truth I am applying to my life is that God wants me to worship in spirit and in truth. Once I have come to the source of spiritual refreshment in a relationship with God through His anointed Messiah, Jesus Christ, I must drink regularly from the well by spiritual and truthful worship. Jesus knows all about me and my past, yet He continually compels me to come to Him. It often seems that He goes out of His way to get my attention and direct me back to this spring of living water.

2. *In Light of the Truth in These Verses, What Changes Must I Make?*

Applying what I've learned in these verses to my personal devotional life, I resolve to make the following changes:

- I will search the Scriptures concerning worship and take my cues from there.
- I resolve to come to God in my quiet times and begin each session with a concentrated time of worship.
- I will thank Him that He has searched my heart and knows me—everything about me—and yet He still loves me. I will ask Him to forgive me for the times I have responded to Him without much depth—frivolously, like the Samaritan woman. After a time of confession of my sins and thanksgiving for His grace, I will gladden His heart by moving on to the next step, which is continual worship.
- I will ask Him to help me bare my heart in praise and

worship. Perhaps I'll recite a psalm or sing a song—or even compose one—that best expresses my heart of praise to God that day.

- I will ask God to help me tell others about His love, even as the Samaritan woman ran to tell the other villagers about her encounter with Jesus. It may mean helping another Christian to learn these same truths or telling an unbeliever about the good news of "living water" in Christ Jesus.

3. *How Will I Carry Out These Changes?*

In my study on worshiping God in spirit and in truth, I might read a psalm that gives me further direction in worship, such as Psalm 95:

> Let us come before His presence with thanksgiving; let us shout joyfully to Him with psalms. For the Lord is the great God, and the great King above all gods. . . . Oh come, let us worship and bow down; let us kneel before the Lord our Maker. . . . Today, if you will hear His voice: "Do not harden your hearts." (VERSES 2-3, 6-8)

When I come before God, I'll thank Him for some specific blessings. I understand how to come into God's presence: to bow down and raise my hands in worship. I know not to harden my heart, but to respond to His voice. When I gather with other believers in fellowship, I'm going to come prepared for worship. Why? Because the Father is seeking those who will worship in spirit and in truth and I want to be one who does just that. I will therefore come with an open heart and an open Bible. I may then call a friend and share the experience I've had with the Lord.

4. *What Will Be My Personal Prayer Concerning This Truth?*

Believing that God has spoken to me in His Word about this specific issue of worship, I want to be sure to respond to Him accordingly:

> Lord, You are so worthy of praise. Forgive me for the lack of praise in my life and change that from today onward. Even as You are seeking those who worship You in spirit and truth, let me be found among those who please You in this manner. Help me not to be concerned with appearances or places, but help my heart to honestly express love to You. Also, Lord, forgive me for all the times I've worshipped at other altars—the broken cisterns of materialism, lust, greed, and self-fulfillment—rather than from Your eternal spring. At those times, I have walked away unsatisfied and thirstier. Quench my eternal thirst through my relationship with You. In Jesus name, Amen.

5. *Which Verse or Verses Should I Memorize?*

I picked verse 24 because it sums up for me the meaning of this text: "God is Spirit, and those who worship Him must worship in spirit and truth." I can easily jot it down, keep it with me to memorize it, and make it the verse I meditate on for the day. (Imagine how much we would benefit if we did this 365 days a year.)

6. *What Illustration or Word Picture Will Help Me Remember What I've Read?*

I picture in my mind two mountains with a man kneeling in between them with his hands raised—and then I cross out the mountains. This reminds me that the external form of our worship is unimportant. Whether we are kneeling on a mountaintop or sitting in a sanctuary is of little significance. The important thing is to have a sincere heart as I worship God.

YOU'RE ON YOUR WAY

This approach to studying the Bible can be used on a daily or weekly basis. The more you do it, the richer the dividends will be. An unknown writer gave this description of the Bible:

> This Book is the mind of God, the state of man, the way of salvation, the doom of sinners, and the happiness of believers. Its doctrines are holy, its precepts are binding; its histories are true, and its decisions are immutable. Read it to be wise, believe it to be safe, practice it to be holy. It contains light to direct you, food to support you, and comfort to cheer you. It is the traveler's map, the pilgrim's staff, the pilot's compass, the soldier's sword, and the Christian's character. Here paradise is restored, heaven opened, and the gates of

> hell disclosed. Christ is its grand subject, our good its design, and the glory of God its end. It should fill the memory, rule the heart, and guide the feet. Read it slowly, frequently, prayerfully. It is a mine of wealth, a paradise of glory, and a river of pleasure. Follow its precepts and it will lead you to Calvary, to the empty tomb, to a resurrected life in Christ; yes, to glory itself, for eternity.[1]

Once you are convinced that the Bible is God's book given for your life, and once you have developed a deep hunger to read it, understand it, and apply it, a whole new world of discovery and enjoyment will be opened up to you. As you practice the principles of observation, interpretation, and application, they will become second nature to you—less mechanical and more enjoyable. Your time in the Word will be more rewarding because you will be able to extract much more truth each time. As you determine to live out these truths, they will transform your life, and Bible study will become, in the words of Jeremiah, "the joy and rejoicing" of your heart (Jeremiah 15:16). There is no other book that compares to the Bible. It stands alone, towering above all others.

Take the book of God's revelation and study it well. As you immerse yourself in the Scriptures, you will grow closer to the divine Author day by day. And what could be more enjoyable than that!

---

[1]INFOsearch: The Communicator's Companion, Illustrations Data and Database, search word "traveler's"; <www.infosearch.com>.

Steps to Peace with God

Step 1 God's Purpose: Peace and Life

God loves you and wants you to experience peace and life—abundant and eternal.

The Bible Says . . .

". . . we have peace with God through our Lord Jesus Christ." Romans 5:1

"For God so loved the world that He gave His only begotten Son, that whoever believes in Him should not perish but have everlasting life." John 3:16

". . . I have come that they may have life, and that they may have it more abundantly." John 10:10b

Since God planned for us to have peace and the abundant life right now, why are most people not having this experience?

Step 2 Our Problem: Separation

God created us in His own image to have an abundant life. He did not make us as robots to automatically love and obey Him, but gave us a will and a freedom of choice.

We chose to disobey God and go our own willful way. We still make this choice today. This results in separation from God.

The Bible Says . . .

"For all have sinned and fall short of the glory of God." Romans 3:23

"For the wages of sin is death, but the gift of God is eternal life in Christ Jesus our Lord." Romans 6:23

Our choice results in separation from God.

Our Attempts

Through the ages, individuals have tried in many ways to bridge this gap . . . without success . . .

The Bible Says . . .

"There is a way that seems right to man, but in the end it leads to death." Proverbs 14:12

"But your iniquities have separated you from God; and your sins have hidden His face from you, so that He will not hear." Isaiah 59:2

There is only one remedy for this problem of separation.

Step 3 God's Remedy: The Cross

Jesus Christ is the only answer to this problem. He died on the Cross and rose from the grave, paying the penalty for our sin and bridging the gap between God and people.

The Bible Says . . .

". . . God is on one side and all the people on the other side, and Christ Jesus, Himself man, is between them to bring them together . . ." 1 Timothy 2:5

"For Christ also has suffered once for sins, the just for the unjust, that He might bring us to God . . ." 1 Peter 3:18a

"But God demonstrates His own love for us in this: While we were still sinners, Christ died for us." Romans 5:8

God has provided the only way . . . we must make the choice . . .

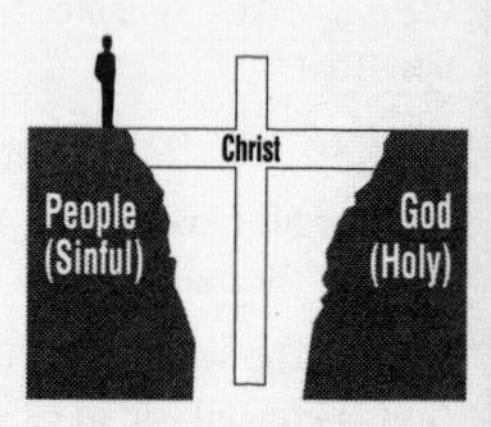

Our Response: Receive Christ

We must trust Jesus Christ and receive Him by personal invitation.

The Bible Says . . .

"Behold, I stand at the door and knock. If anyone hears My voice and opens the door, I will come in to him and dine with him, and he with Me." Revelation 3:20

"But as many as received Him, to them He gave the right to become children of God, even to those who believe in His name." John 1:12

". . . if you confess with your mouth the Lord Jesus and believe in your heart that God has raised Him from the dead, you will be saved." Romans 10:9

Are you here . . . or here?

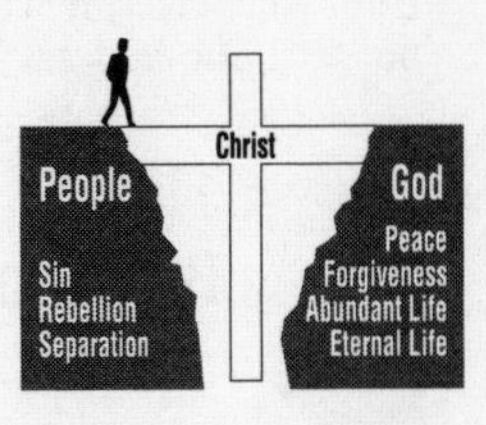

Is there any good reason why you cannot receive Jesus Christ right now?

How to receive Christ:

1. Admit your need (I am a sinner).
2. Be willing to turn from your sins (repent).
3. Believe that Jesus Christ died for you on the Cross and rose from the grave.
4. Through prayer, invite Jesus Christ to come in and control your life through the Holy Spirit. (Receive Him as Lord and Savior.)

What to Pray:

Dear Lord Jesus,

I know that I am a sinner and need Your forgiveness. I believe that You died for my sins. I want to turn from my sins. I now invite You to come into my heart and life. I want to trust and follow You as Lord and Savior.

In Jesus' name. Amen.

________________ Date

____________________________ Signature

God's Assurance: His Word

If you prayed this prayer,

The Bible Says...

"For 'whoever calls upon the name of the Lord will be saved.'" Romans 10:13

Did you sincerely ask Jesus Christ to come into your life? Where is He right now? What has He given you?

"For it is by grace you have been saved, through faith—and this is not from yourselves, it is the gift of God—not by works, so that no one can boast." Ephesians 2:8,9

The Bible Says...

"He who has the Son has life; he who does not have the Son of God does not have life. These things I have written to you who believe in the name of the Son of God, that you may know that you have eternal life, and that you may continue to believe in the name of the Son of God." 1 John 5:12–13, NKJV

Receiving Christ, we are born into God's family through the supernatural work of the Holy Spirit who indwells every believer...this is called regeneration or the "new birth."

This is just the beginning of a wonderful new life in Christ. To deepen this relationship you should:

1. Read your Bible every day to know Christ better.
2. Talk to God in prayer every day.
3. Tell others about Christ.
4. Worship, fellowship, and serve with other Christians in a church where Christ is preached.
5. As Christ's representative in a needy world, demonstrate your new life by your love and concern for others.

God bless you as you do.

Billy Graham

If you want further help in the decision you have made, write to:
Billy Graham Evangelistic Association P.O. Box 779, Minneapolis, Minnesota 55440-0779

If you are committing your life to Christ, please let us know! We would like to send you Bible study materials and a complimentary six-month subscription to *Decision* magazine to help you grow in your faith.

The Billy Graham Evangelistic Association exists to support the evangelistic ministry and calling of Billy Graham to take the message of Christ to all we can by every prudent means available to us.

Our desire is to introduce as many as we can to the person of Jesus Christ, so that they might experience His love and forgiveness.

Your prayers are the most important way to support us in this ministry. We are grateful for the dedicated prayer support we receive. We are also grateful for those that support us with contributions.

Giving can be a rewarding experience for you and for us at the Billy Graham Evangelistic Association (BGEA). Your gift gives you the satisfaction of supporting an organization that is actively involved in evangelism. Also, it is encouraging to us because part of our ministry is devoted to helping people like you discover and enjoy the stewardship of giving wisely and effectively.

Billy Graham Evangelistic Association
P.O. Box 779
Minneapolis, Minnesota 55440-0779
www.billygraham.org

Billy Graham Evangelistic Association of Canada
P.O. Box 841, Stn Main
Winnipeg, Manitoba R3C 2R3
www.billygraham.ca

Toll free: 1-877-247-2426